# THE LOST FILMS

## FEATURES

**THE KING KONG REMAKE THAT BECAME A CAR COMMERCIAL** Learn how David Allen's color King Kong test footage for Hammer turned into a VW ad in 1972...7

**THE TERROR OF TERREMOTO 10 GRADO!!!** This lost cut of Legend of Dinosaurs and Monster Birds has been missing for years. is it better than the original?...10

**GOOD LUCK! GODZILLA** Toho's secret 1967 monster movie that you can watch right now. if you know where to look...23

**"IF IT HAD BEEN IN COLOR WE'D HAVE HAD A BIG HIT!"** Merian C. Cooper's 1935 adaptations of She and The Last Days of Pompeii were meant to be the next King Kong. What went wrong?...27

**AATANK ATTACKS!** Discover the Bollywood version of Jaws that went unfinished for years...30

**IMITATION SPAGHETTI** Meet Paul Coby and Michael Smith. the men who mimicked Terence Hill and Bud Spencer...34

**BRIDE OF DR. PHIBES!** Thrill to the first crack at Phibes #2. which almost became Phibes #3...39

**THE TOP 10 BEST GODZILLA FAN TRAILERS** The best of the best Godzilla fan trailers ranked...43

**INTERVIEW WITH SCOTT DAVID LISTER** You just read about the trailers. now meet the maker of three of the very best...56

---

THE LOST FILMS FANZINE, VOL. 1, #1 SPRING 2020

EDITOR AND PUBLISHER: JOHN LEMAY  SPECIAL CONSULTANT: KYLE BYRD
SPECIAL THANKS THIS ISSUE TO MAX DELLA MORA & SCOTT DAVID LISTER

THE LOST FILMS FANZINE IS PUBLISHED FOUR TIMES A YEAR. THE COPYRIGHTS AND TRADEMARKS OF THE IMAGES FEATURED THEREIN ARE HELD BY THEIR RESPECTIVE OWNERS. THE LOST FILMS FANZINE ACKNOWLEDGES THE RIGHTS OF THE CREATORS AND THE COPYRIGHT HOLDERS OF THE IMAGES THEREIN AND DOES NOT SEEK TO INFRINGE UPON THOSE RIGHTS. ARTICLES WITHIN THE MAGAZINE ARE © THEIR RESPECTIVE AUTHORS AND MAY NOT BE REPRINTED WITHOUT PERMISSION.

---

If y
ask
wo
starters, I like fanzines and have written for quite a few. *G-Fan*, *Xenorama*, *Mad Scientist*, and *Cinema Retro* are all some of my favorites. But, often I find things I want to write about that escapes the scope of my books or the pages of *G-Fan* and the other aforementioned 'zines (which I still plan to write for, by the way).

You can also blame this on quarantine boredom as COVID-19 is still in full swing. Like so many others, I got a little stir crazy and decided to do something creative, in this case, finally go for my own fanzine, which is something I've debated doing for the past several years. Naturally, this fanzine is devoted to what has become my calling card in recent years: lost films. If you've read my books, you know I hang pretty loose with what defines a "lost film." In my case that could mean an unproduced script (Peter Seller's *Romance of the Pink Panther*), a film that's literally been destroyed (1938's *King Kong Appears in Edo*), or even a rare hard to find film (Bollywood's *Aatank*) could fall under that category. I mean, really, isn't anything lost if you haven't found it yet? So while *Aatank* has existed in some form for years now, it might've been "lost" to you personally until now.

Furthermore, I should specify this fanzine will focus on lost genre films. Things like F.W. Murnau's *4 Devils* or unmade sequels to *Citizen Kane* you will most likely never find here. I also have an affinity for older lost films, and while the news section might report on new productions like *Great Buddha Arrival*, most of what you'll find here will come from the 1940s through the 1970s, though occasionally I might stray into the 1980s or 1990s, but probably not the 2000s.

Whether you agree with my criteria or not, I hope you enjoy exploring the films that could have been, as well as those still out there that you might have missed...

John LeMay

# NEWS

Posters for *Nezura 1964* (left) and *Monster Seafood Wars* (right).

## LOST NO MORE! TWO "LOST" TOKUSATSU FILMS REVIVED!!!

First, the lost 1934 film *The Giant Buddha Statue's Travel Through the Country* was "remade," in a manner of speaking, as *Great Buddha Arrival* in 2018. That film's producer, Avery Guerra, is now working with Kadokawa to revive another lost film: *Giant Horde Beast Nezura*. The 1964 Daiei film was about giant rats invading Tokyo, and was shut down due to the difficulties of using live rats on a miniature Tokyo set. The new film will be called *Nezura 1964*. When asked if it would be similar in style to *Great Buddha Arrival*, Guerra said, "It's a meta film much like *The Great Buddha Arrival*. It's about the troubles of the making of the film but also will show imagined finished sequences of the film."

Another film, currently in post-production, took inspiration from an even older source: an early idea of Eiji Tsuburaya. The father of Japanese SPFX had long held an affinity for giant octopi and wrote a story treatment where a giant octopus begins sinking ships in the Indian Ocean. It makes its way to Japan, where it is killed at the foot of Mt. Fuji with a top secret weapon: the vinegar gun! The giant octopus is then distributed as food as a way of solving the post-WWII food shortage. Filmmaker Minoru Kawasaki (*The World Sinks Except Japan; The Calamari Wrestler*) took the old story as inspiration to make *Monster Seafood Wars*, which also seems to spoof *Space Amoeba* (1970) as it features a cuttlefish and a crab kaiju.

The film was supposed to premiere in Japan on May 23, 2020. It's unknown if it will still do so due to the recent outbreak of COVID-19. Look for updates next issue!

# Grizzly II Premieres!

We're happy to announce that the sequel to 1976's *Grizzly*, called *Grizzly II*, was able to premiere in Los Angeles in February before the COVID-19 quarantine. *Grizzly II* is a rare example of a film that shut down in the middle of shooting and resumed years later. Enough footage was captured during principal photography in 1983 to salvage the movie 35 years later!

On the film's official website, producer Suzanne Nagy wrote, "In 2018, the time was right to rethink the *Grizzly* movie and create a challenging new narrative with a new message which could fill the missing part in the movie. Restoring the old footage was a great challenge. But in the summer of 2019, we got a clean, super crispy digital transfer from London. During the waiting period, we worked on the new script and re-erected the film from its dormant stage. We didn't want to make a 21st century movie when we looked at the footage. We wanted to keep it as original as possible to have an authentic American movie quality from the 80's. Something that was missed or lost and found later on to attract enthusiastic cult lovers."

Though it has alternatively been subtitled as *Grizzly II: The Predator* and others times as *The Concert* (the bear attacks a rock concert), the final version has been subtitled "Revenge". After the film completes its circuit on film festivals, it will hopefully secure a DVD/Blu-Ray release.

# NEWS BRIEFS

**FUTURE LOST FILM? GODZILLA ONE MILLION YEARS B.C.???**
During a recent watch party for *Godzilla: King of the Monsters* (2019) director Mike Dougherty tweeted that, "I'd still love to do GODZILLA B.C. where we finally see this ancient world of man and monster, like a modern-day Ray Harryhausen flick. Or maybe we just go for it and finally take humans out of the equation."

Before this, Dougherty had stated, "I like the idea of going back in time and telling creatures' stories from different eras. *Skull Island* was set in the '70s, but personally I'd like to do *Godzilla B.C.*, go back to ancient times and really see the Ray Harryhausen-esque world where primitive humans had to try to survive with these creatures. Maybe we'd get to see the first time mankind truly encountered Godzilla, and get to see how that relationship was christened."

However, even if *Godzilla vs. Kong* manages to be a hit when it's released, it's highly unlikely that there will be a "Godzilla B.C." film. That all said, I think it would make for a great prequel comic! The Shobojin wearing Raquel Welch-style fur bikinis anyone?

## JAWS REMAKE ON THE WAY?

Though we've heard this before, allegedly Universal is pondering a *Jaws* remake. Whereas in the early 2000s there were rumors of direct-to-DVD sequels, the word remake started getting tossed around in 2010 (comedian Tracy Morgan was even rumored for the Hooper role). Will these latest whispers ever come to fruition, or are they nothing more than rumors? Time will tell.

**STAR WARS SCRIPT LEAK** Star Wars fans divided by the love it or hate it reaction to *The Last Jedi* were united this past Christmas over their mutual dislike of *The Rise of Skywalker*. The original version of Episode IX was to be directed by *Jurassic World's* Colin Trevorrow before he was replaced by J.J. Abrams. Luckily, Trevorrow's Star Wars Episode IX script, subtitled *Duel of the Fates*, has leaked and by all accounts seems to be better liked than the final product.

Among the more interesting ideas were to have Chewie piloting an X-wing during the final battle, said to take place over Coruscant. There was no forced resurrection of Emperor Palpatine, and Kylo Ren would have trained under a former Sith master of Darth Sidious (NOT Darth Plagueis though).

Had Trevorrow not been let go, it's doubtful the movie would have been filmed as scripted due to the death of Carrie Fisher, who was still alive at the time of its writing.

**LOST FILMS LEGEND PASSES** We are saddened to report on the passing of director Nobuhiko Obayashi, who many will remember as the director of *House* (1977). Lost film fans will always remember him for his wild-aborted Godzilla movie, *A Space Godzilla*, published in the Japanese *Starlog* in 1979. RIP Mr. Obayashi!

**ORIGINAL *ALIEN* SCRIPT COMIC ADAPTATION DROPS** Courtesy of Dark Horse Comics comes an adaptation of the original screenplay of *Alien* by Dan O'Bannon, which notably did not feature Ripley. The five issue miniseries is adapted by writer Cristiano Seixas and artist Guilherme Balbi.

**GAPPA ANGRY! TOKYO SHOCK BLU-RAY ALREADY OUT OF PRINT?** Bad news Gappa fans, Tokyo Shock's Blu-Ray release of *Gappa, the Triphibian Monster* (1967) is already out of print. My introduction to Gappa came via the old Orion VHS of *Monster from a Prehistoric Planet*. Though I liked it, I wasn't wild about Gappa, and it wasn't a title I revisited often. However, watching Tokyo Shock's Blu-Ray was almost like seeing the film for the first time. The print was stellar, and the audio was crisp. Though you can't get a new one any longer, I'd grab it now from third party sellers before prices skyrocket any higher.

# THE KING KONG REMAKE

## THAT BECAME A VOLKSWAGEN COMMERCIAL

In the late 1960s, a *King Kong* color remake was on the minds of several different producers. Kong's original producer/creator Merian C. Cooper had his own far-out idea to remake King Kong in outer space! (Don't believe me? It's in the Merian C. Cooper papers kept at Brigham Young University.) In England, Hammer Films wanted to do something special for their upcoming 100th production... which would, in fact, not be their 100th production, that was just a publicity stunt.

Hammer had ideas of remaking *King Kong* in either 1965 or 1966, but when they approached RKO, who still held the rights to Kong, they said they would only allow sequels along the lines of *King Kong vs. Godzilla* (1962). Hammer gave up for the time being and decided to remake Hal Roache's *One Million B.C.* (1940). Rather than use lizards disguised as dinosaurs like the original did, Hammer hired Ray Harryhausen to create stopmotion prehistoric monsters. The film was retitled *One Million Years B.C.* and was released in 1966 to great success (as their "100th" Film"). A sequel, *When Dinosaurs Ruled the Earth*, came out in 1970, and it too was a hit. This apparently inspired Hammer try at remaking *King Kong* again in stopmotion. David Allen, an assistant animator on *When Dinosaurs Ruled the Earth*, heard talk of the project and took it upon himself to create some color test footage for the prospective remake.

Allen constructed a 12" model that was identical to the original Kong constructed by Marcel Delgado back in 1933. Next, Allen constructed a miniature set of the Empire Studio at Cascade Pictures in California. There he shot four scenes at his own expense. When

7/THE LOST FILMS FANZINE #1

remake rights again. The project was dead.

Thankfully, this wasn't the end of Allen's Kong footage, though. He decided to use it as what we might today call a "demo reel." He sent out his Kong test footage for the cancelled remake to different ad agencies as an example of what he was capable of. Lucky for him, the early 1970s was nostalgic for the 1920s and 1930s. In only three months, his footage caught the eye of an advertising firm currently trying to come up with a way to market Volkswagen's new, larger "super-bug." The executives decided that using a monster to demonstrate the vehicle's size would be a novel idea.

Initially, Allen wasn't even the first choice for the commercial (remember, all he shot was Kong atop the Empire State Building, new scenes would be needed too). Various production companies bid on the project, but they would have simply used the man-in-suit approach. The executives were smart enough to finally hire Allen himself to finish the commercial. The executives even cast Fay Wray's daughter, Vickie Riskin, as Kong's girlfriend! Though most of the commercial would be stop motion, there were a few scenes that only needed to show Kong's hand. For those it was decided to use a man wearing an ape glove. The man hired was none other than Rick Baker, the very man who would create and don the ape suit in the 1976 *King Kong* remake! Baker was Allen's suggestion, but Allen's bosses had suggested two performers before Baker. George Barrows, who had infamously portrayed the title characters in 1954's *Gorilla at Large* and 1961's *Konga* was the first choice, and a lesser known ape performer, Janos

the footage was finished, he dubbed in the soundtrack and effects of the 1933 original. Allen showed Hammer his 35 mm print, but it was no use. RKO had denied Hammer

Prohaska. Barrows wasn't interested, and Prohaska asked for too much money. Allen was right again, and Baker was hired. Little could Baker imagine that one day he'd play the famous ape again in an even greater capacity!

Production lasted around one month. Though the original Allen footage was not used as sometimes reported (heck, I think I've even been guilty of that!), Allen's original Kong model was animated by him again for the commercial, codenamed "Fay's Friend."

The hilarious commercial had Kong battling the biplanes atop the Empire State Building. He catches one of the planes, but something down below has caught his eye. He tucks the biplane under his arm and climbs down the building, his "girlfriend" still in hand. On the street, Kong inspects the new VW 411, and places the small beauty in the passenger seat, while he puts the biplane in the trunk. The duo drive off together in what essentially amounted to the Super Bowl Commercial of its day. Sadly, its charms were not appreciated at the time. (Don't get confused, I'm not saying it aired during a Super Bowl, I'm saying it was the type of big-budget, high concept commercial we associate with Super Bowls today).

Audiences loved the commercial. They loved it so much that VW pulled it after only about three airings! In the VW ad executives' minds, Kong either distracted from the car or made a mockery of it. Some feared that impressionable viewers might think that the car really was huge—maybe not as huge as King Kong—but still bigger than they might be comfortable with. Lamer excuses went that executives didn't like the idea of an ape driving the car, and another said that Kong had frightened his daughter!!!

In recent years, VW has atoned for their sins and created another King Kong commercial. In this one, a giant inflatable gorilla at a car lot notices a Volkswagen Tiguan and decides to chase it through New York. Both VW Kong commercials can be found online if one wants to see them.

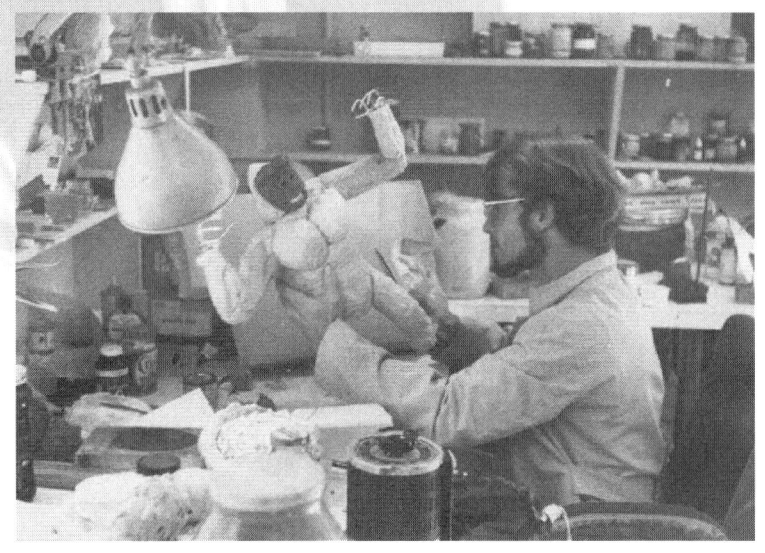

**David Allen and Kong c.1970.**

9/THE LOST FILMS FANZINE #1

NELLA SUGGESTIONE DEL MAGICSOU…

# TERREMOTO
## 10° GRADO

con SUNEHIKO WATASE · DAVID FREEDMAN · SHOTARO HAYASH · JASMIN WA…

## TERROR OF TERREMOTO 10 GRADO!!!
## LEGEND OF THE DINOSAURS LIKE YOU'VE NEVER SEEN IT BEFORE!!!

Legend of Dinosaurs and Monster Birds © 1977 Toei.

By now, fans are used to misleading European posters for their favorite kaiju-eiga. Case in point, Italy's *Il Ritorno di Gorgo* (1976), which features a giant, clawed hand as big as the battleship it's about to destroy. As it turned out, not only was the titular monster not that big, but the titular monster was Godzilla. The distributors had simply decided to rerelease 1967's *Son of Godzilla* as though it was a *Gorgo* sequel. What a gyp, right?

But, want to hear something shocking about the Italian release for Toei's *Legend of Dinosaurs and Monster Birds*? The poster for the film, renamed *Terremoto 10 Grado* (*Magnitude 10 Earthquake*), isn't all that misleading. It's got two pteranodons compared to the film's sole Rhamphorynchus, true, but even the Japanese poster was guilty of that sin. It's also got helicopters and an erupting volcano. But, John, you say, *Legend of Dinosaurs* does not have cities erupting into flame! Or tidal waves! You're right. *Legend of Dinosaurs* doesn't, but *Terremoto 10 Grado* does.

To backtrack just a bit, Toei's *Legend of Dinosaurs and Monster Birds* was shot in late 1976 to capitalize on the hype from *Jaws*, released in Japan in December of 1975. *Legend* was Toei's most expensive production to date (allegedly), and the studio was so confident that it would be a hit that the trailer proclaimed that the film would see release in 40 territories. But, when the film opened in Japan in April of 1977, it was a monumental flop.

Toei apparently managed to keep this a semi-secret in the press, or at least as far as I can tell they did. Looking through old magazines like *House of Hammer* and *Castle of Frankenstein,* I saw many positive mentions of the film. *House of Hammer* #19, for instance, claimed that *Legend* cost $2.5 million to make and that it would make its international premiere at the 1978 Fantasy Film Festival in Paris. Other sources tell me it premiered at a U.S.

II/THE LOST FILMS FANZINE #1

screening for potential distributers on October 12, 1977.

Though the U.S. was probably Toei's #1 target when it came to international distribution, the film wouldn't see release there until the early 1980s. And even then, that was only on cable TV and video rental shelves via Sandy Frank, who had the audacity to publish this gore-fest under their "Just For Kids" label.

*Legend* received theatrical distribution in Germany, France, Italy, and South America that we know of. But it's uncertain how it actually performed. The only place we know of for certain where *Legend* was a hit was the Soviet Union. It wasn't because they loved kaiju-eiga though, they had never even seen one. *Legend* was, for whatever reason, the first Japanese monster film of its kind released in that country. And that still wasn't the main reason it was a hit (Russian audiences were primarily intrigued by the film because it depicted a capitalist Asian country). Let this sink in for a moment: the film was such a hit that *Godzilla vs. Mechagodzilla II* (1993) was retitled *Legend of the Dinosaurs 2* in Russia! I mean it does have a big dinosaur egg and a pteranodon in it...

But, we're not here to talk about the Russian version, which I have seen, and it's not that interesting. Aside from snipping a few scenes here and there, redoing the titles, etc. there's not much difference between *Legend of Dinosaurs and Monster Birds* and *Legend of Dinosaurs* as they call it. But Italy's *Terremoto 10 Grado* is a different story compared to all the other foreign releases of the movie. For starters, it gives the film an entirely new soundtrack (which Germany and France also did, but not to this extent, trust me!) *Terremoto 10 Grado* also reshuffles scenes, adds in footage, and it has an alternate ending. You read that right.

It's not exactly *Godzilla, King of the Monsters* with Raymond Burr, there are no new characters or protagonists. But, there is a new subplot with stock footage to back it up. If anything, *Terremoto 10 Grado* is probably the most comparable to the U.S. re-edits of *Ghidorah/Ghidrah, the Three-Headed Monster* and *Day of Resurrection/Virus*.

Unfortunately, I can find no concrete release date for *Terremoto 10 Grado* in Italy, but presumably it was released sometime between 1977 and 1980. As for the title, 1974's *Earthquake* had been a big hit in Italy. Naturally, it was called *Terremoto*. So the distributors apparently were trying to pass off *Legend* as either a sequel or a topper to *Earthquake*, as this film would be called *Magnitude 10 Earthquake*.

As an unabashed proponent of *Legend of Dinosaur's* greatness, I prided myself on having seen the various versions of the movie, which up until *Terremoto* included *Giants of the Past* (Germany), *Monsters of Prehistory* (France), and *Legend of Dinosaurs* (Russia). Nothing could have prepared me for *Terremoto* though.

I was introduced to this cut via a clip posted on Facebook, which featured the raft scene rescored with John Barry's theme from *The Deep* (1977). It definitely made the scene creepier than it already was, but I had no idea how *Terremoto* altered *Legend* in other ways. As I began to dig around, I found one post in Italian that gave a fairly accurate synopsis of the film aside from mention of an asteroid causing calamity on Earth. I took this to be a rumor or error in translation.

# TERREMOTO
## 10º GRADO

SUMEKUKO WATASE · DAVID FREEDMAN · SHOTARO HAYASHI · JASMIN WAHAB
JURIJ KURATA
TOEI COMPANY LTD

UNIFILM DISTRIBUZIONE presenta
TERREMOTO
10° GRADO
WATASE · DAVID FREEDMAN · SHOTARO HAYASH · JASMIN WAHAB
KURATA
TOEI COMPANY LTD
EASTMANCOLOR

In talking to a friend, Max Della Mora, about *Terremoto,* he told me he had an old PAL VHS with that cut of the film and offered to show me a digital transfer of it. I was astounded by what I saw. The rumors about the satellite subplot were true and then some.

Before delving into all the differences, I think some discussion on the rescoring of the movie is in order. Fans of *Legend* are usually also fans of its unique—many would say misplaced—score by Masao Yagi. I am one of them. The Rhamphorynchus's funky dance theme as it slaughters the villagers is one in a million. However, by overlaying *Legend* with the score from *The Deep* (plus a few other scores that I presume to be from Italian horror flicks), the film takes on a slightly more serious—dare I even say epic?—feel. *The Deep's* John Barry was best known for scoring the Bond films, but in 1976 he had also scored *King Kong.* So, in large part, Barry's lifted tracks are to thank for making *Terremoto* such an interesting experience. The music even helps the monsters come across more seriously (yes, even a super fan like me can admit that they are bad).

Any true *Legend* fan can spot the differences in *Terremoto* right away, as this cut bypasses the first shots of the film. Whereas *Legend* begins with a suicidal woman wandering through Aokigahara forest and falling into an ice cave, *Terremoto* opens inside the ice cave. There we find an unconscious woman just beginning to stir. But how did she get there? A quick POV shot of her looking up at the hole pretty well explains to the viewer that she's fallen in.

The scene, unscored in *Legend*, is scored here with an unknown Italian horror track that is quite effective. The woman takes note of a gigantic egg and stumbles towards it. Inside she spies a grotesque, giant eye and screams in horror. We fade out on the giant eye, and then cut away to an underwater abyss where the title credits roll (*Legend's* credits don't play until after Ashizawa gets fired by his boss).

When the credits end, we're in all-new territory (i.e., footage unique to *Terremoto*) as a newscast reveals to us that the world is in a state of turmoil. Stock special effects shots and newsreel footage of real disasters play. I'm not sure where most of them come from, but at least one I recognized to be from the ending tidal wave from *When Dinosaurs Ruled the Earth* (1970). Other notable scenes included a dam breaking (no, it wasn't from *Superman: The Movie*, I checked).

We cut to Ashizawa's introductory scene at the airport, where he's supposed to board a flight to Mexico (as a geologist, he's supposed to investigate some new finds in the Yucatan). Just then, another news bulletin comes on explaining the source of the recent calamity. According to the newscaster, an asteroid struck the NASA satellite Saturn 10 (a few effects shots from an unknown production are glimpsed too).

Now, is the newscaster implying the asteroid first struck the satellite and then struck Earth? That isn't exactly clear, nor is it explicitly stated, but that would make the most sense, as an asteroid striking a satellite wouldn't cause earthquakes on Earth! I also wonder if the new writers were trying to draw a connection between this new asteroid and the one that wiped out the dinosaurs—the irony here being that perhaps an asteroid has awakened the dinosaurs.

15/THE LOST FILMS FANZINE #1

*New title card for Terremoto 10 Grado.*

*One of the Italian newscasters.*

*Footage of a dam breaking from an unknown film.*

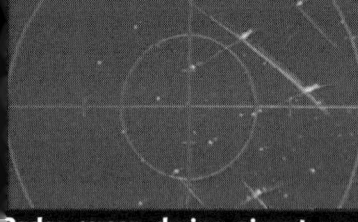

*Radar screen during airport news report on the satellite.*

*Image of satellite shortly before it explodes into a ball of light.*

The broadcast catches Ashizawa's eye, and he's already on his way out of the airport when they switch to their next segment, covering the woman who found the stone egg. In another alteration unique to *Terremoto*, this newscast also covers the upcoming dragon festival at Lake Sai, something that *Legend* never does via the newscast. The scene of the girl being pronounced dead at the hospital is cut, but we do see Ashizawa talking to someone about the girl over a payphone outside the airport.

If you remember *Legend*, you'll know that Ashizawa's annoying co-worker comes outside and tells him to hurry up and get back inside. Ashizawa tells the guy to stick it and goes off to see his boss at Universal Stone Co... in *Legend* at least. In *Terremoto*, Ashizawa goes to see a professor friend at the meteorological institute (in *Legend*, this scene doesn't occur until later in the film). The duo talks about earthquakes, and suddenly Ashizawa is speeding down the Tokyo freeway out of town (but sans the Japanese credits and power ballad, of course).

Ashizawa's scene with the three youths when he first pulls into the village near Lake Sai is removed. In *Terremoto*, we go straight to his scene exploring Aokigahara. Aside from the removal of the Japanese ballad, which is replaced with a more appropriate score, the scene plays out normally. But, just when I thought that this cut might settle into a more predictable groove, it shocked me again. As the earthquake progresses, the ground splits open, and lava spews into the air! The movie is blowing its load early, way early... as in showing footage from the climactic eruption at less than twenty minutes in.

However, this traumatic tremor doesn't do Ashizawa in; he still awakens in Muku's cabin (Muku is the old friend of Ashizawa's father if you'll recall). Now, whereas a lot of foreign edits might have let the new earthquake scene disappear as mysteriously as it appeared, *Terremoto* isn't messing around. Sounds of a distant volcanic eruption can be heard in the background as the two men talk (if the Italian dialogue reflects these changes is something I'd like to know). I was impressed with the movie's commitment to heightening the disaster aspect of the story, and the sounds of a distant eruption are dubbed into many other scenes as well.

The movie progresses normally for a while, only when we see Akiko and Junko scuba diving they are accompanied by John Barry's excellent theme from *The Deep*. Later, Ashizawa bumps into the girls, renamed Angie and Julie, on the lakeshore, and goes back to Angie's motorhome with her. He puts the moves on Angie inside, and the duo presumably gets it on. I say presumably because *Terremoto* removes the end of the scene. In *Legend*, the mood is ruined when Akiko spots a mass of snakes (or are they eels?) that have somehow wormed their way into the motorhome.

The plesiosaur's first kill scene also receives a major overhaul. In *Legend* it's killing of a couple on a paddleboat is revealed through sound effects only, building up some mystery. *Terremoto* blows its load again by editing in snippets of footage from later in the film where it kills the two hoaxers! We don't see the dinosaur's head, but we do see its tail thrash the couple (really just quick shots of the two male hoaxers).

**Newly inserted shot of "Mt. Fuji" that precedes Ashizawa's arrival at Lake Sai.**

**"New" reversed shot of plesiosaur.**

**Switchboard operators take calls after Junko's death scene.**

**Newscaster reports on Junko's death.**

**The suicidal woman from the movie's opening doubles as the woman eaten by the dinosaur in the cabin in a repeated shot.**

**Publicity still of Junko and the Plesiosaur.** Legend of Dinosaurs and Monster Birds © 1977 Toei.

The movie continued to throw me for a loop as the next scene had Ashizawa back in Tokyo talking to his boss. I had assumed that the scene was cut entirely, but no, they decided to place it here for some reason.

Next up, Ashizawa is driving "back" into Lake Sai (remember, in *Legend* once he gets there he never leaves) when he comes across a screaming Julie/Junko. She has discovered the body of a headless horse in a pool of blood. As Italians love their gore, you can rest assured that no gore was cut, though for some reason, the shot of her screaming in the puddle of blood was shortened.

As in *Legend*, the next day the dragon festival commences. In this dub, Akira Moroguchi (the country singer) is singing "I've Got the Tiger By the Tail" and later "King of the Road"! This movie obviously didn't worry about music royalties. The festival scene is re-edited, but not in any way really worth discussing—just the removal of a little shot here and there to tighten the pacing.

The plesiosaur's killing of the two hoaxers in front of their friend is intact but uses creepy music from *The Deep* in place of Yagi's jazzy score.

The distraught friend tries to tell the authorities about the monster, but considering he was compliant in the hoax earlier, they dismiss his claims. Then the reporter Harold Tucker busts inside with his infamous line about how "Nessie's in Lake Sai!" and "It's super big news!" We cut to a new shot of lava shooting into the night sky. Wait, what? Shouldn't we be watching the plesiosaur eat that woman in the cabin right about now?

*Terremoto* decides to save the dinosaur rampage for later. We cut to the friend of the two dead men at a bonfire at the lake. He is drunk and calling two divers cowards for not diving to look for the monster. They get angry and knock him into the lake. The scene, which in *Legend* takes place about 20 minutes from where it is placed in *Terremoto*, ends with the man crying and then cuts to a photo of the Loch Ness Monster. We are now in yet another scene that should be taking place after the dino killing spree, not before it. Harold Tucker, the reporter, is comparing the Lake Sai monster to Nessie in a town hall meeting (meant to mimic a similar scene from *Jaws*). Remember, in *Legend*, this meeting is being held because several people are dead. In this cut, only the two hoaxers have been killed, and the claim that the monster ate them is doubted by the officials.

The scene has an effective new ending, though. After a professor says that conditions are right for a cataclysmic earthquake, we cut to new footage of a volcano exploding. Then we cut to shots of dark clouds spreading above the straw dragon effigy on the lakeshore (a scene from much later in *Legend*). Coupled with ominous music, it's an effective transition that foreshadows that something very bad is about to happen.

Cut to Akiko... err, Angie, diving into Lake Sai (no, the plesiosaur still hasn't eaten the woman in the cabin) and poor Junko/Julie, is all alone in the raft. As the scene of Junko interviewing the old woman was cut, Julie, therefore, cannot listen to the old woman's folksong on the raft. Instead, she listens to a radio report for a moment before switching it off.

We all know what happens next. The sequence is re-edited slightly, but only for pacing, not for gore. Played out to the theme from *The Deep*, the scene is very creepy, possibly scarier than the version we get in *Legend*. As in *Legend*, the last we see of poor Julie is her struggling to keep her head above water as the monster looks on. Angie returns to the raft to find the radio on, but no Julie. A hand clasps at the raft, and Angie pulls her friend in, or part of her at least. The famous torso scene cut from the U.S. version for its shock factor is retained here.

The ensuing media frenzy and search for the monster is all over the place in *Terremoto*. Only a maniac like me would be interested in all the little deviations, so I'll spare you the details. What's important to know is that this is the portion of the movie where the dinosaur kills the woman in the cabin.

As to why this is, I assume it's because the producers wanted to stress that the plesiosaur wasn't in the lake during the search. The cabin scene is a doozy of a re-edit too. From a shot of an underwater camera sinking into the lake, we cut to a POV shot from the plesiosaur's perspective as it plods through the forest. It spies a cabin. Inside, a woman is taking a shower.

Though I wouldn't have thought the Italians would have anything against a quick nude shot in a late 1970's gore flick, for whatever reason, the quick shot of the woman in the shower is removed. The scene's re-edit is much better than the original thanks to the new suspenseful score for starters. Sounds of the dinosaur breathing are also added. Removed is a horrid shot of the monster's head outside the window that creates a shoddy error in scale, too.

Despite that cut, the scene is actually extended by inserting shots of the plesiosaur in the forest from the ending of the film. This makes is appear as though the monster is peeping in at her through the windows longer. As the woman is putting on a shirt, she finally takes note of the monster's loud breathing. She turns and the dinosaur's head bursts through the wall. But it's not over yet.

The sequence has a different ending by way of showing the

19/THE LOST FILMS FANZINE #1

**Still from the film's ending at Mt. Fuji.** Legend of Dinosaurs and Monster Birds © 1977 Toei.

woman screaming. This is accomplished via a quick repeat shot of the suicidal woman from Aokigahara forest screaming at the egg in the film's opening scene! It's a very effective cut when coupled with the downbeat music and the woman's screams, which we can still hear when we transition to the next shot of a radar screen at the Monster Search HQ.

One of the scenes to follow this one is Ashizawa and "Angie" at the cabin. You know, the one where he slaps her during an argument. The scene is made all the more tense by the addition of sound effects of Mt. Fuji rumbling in the distance.

The sequence of events from here on out doesn't deviate much from *Legend*. At least no major scenes are moved around, but plenty of shots are changed up for varying reasons, notably when depth charges are dropped in the lake when Ashizawa goes scuba diving.

As Angie sees him off into the depths, something suddenly catches her attention. In *Legend*, it is a loudspeaker announcing the depth charges. But in *Terremoto*, it is an exploding caldera. It's implied that this explosion also knocked Muku into a cave. Muku, in case you don't remember, is exploring Aokigahara along with the reporter, Akira, who somehow knows that a pterodactyl will show up later.

Speaking of monster birds, the hatching of the Rhamphorynchus takes place earlier in this cut, and it's also edited a bit. Akira and Muku's exploration of the melting ice cave is interspersed with random shots of volcanic activity. At one point, Muku shouts, "Earthquake!" This doesn't happen in *Legend*, where there's no real discussion of earthquakes on Muku's part. But don't worry, the gore is intact and the monster bird makes one heck of an entrance. But whereas *Legend* cuts from the

20/THE LOST FILMS FANZINE #1

chattering beak coming out of the egg to Akiko and Ashizawa making their way up a waterfall, *Terremoto* cuts to the loudspeaker announcing that depth charges are about to be dropped in the lake. Angie/Akiko listens to the news and rushes home. As you can see, in *Legend,* the bird hatches well after the lovers are in the lake together, but here it happens before.

There aren't any real interesting changes to discuss as to Angie rescuing Ashizawa other than *The Deep* theme is used in those scenes, and it's magnificent. Also, when Ashizawa spots a floating head in the water, *Terremoto* repeats the shot of the head and Ashizawa's reaction. While *Legend* cuts to Muku's fall from here, *Terremoto* had already done that. *Terremoto* cuts to a rather distinct shot of the "earthquake lights." You know what that means, the monster bird is about to make its big entrance and kill the villagers. And it does so uncut and unedited—aside from its groovy theme song being removed for a different track. As inappropriate as Yagi's score for that scene was, you just almost can't help but miss it. Though more appropriate, the new score somewhat lacks the momentum.

The ending scenes in Aokigihara forest when Mt. Fuji erupts are improved in several different ways. For starters, when Ashizawa and Angie emerge from the cave into the forest, some new, hopeful sounding music plays. The new score used upon the entrance of the plesiosaur is also well done.

When the monster fight begins, *Terremoto* has the good sense to remove an awful overhead shot of the monster bird where it looks like an escaped museum prop jiggled from a wire. It removes another shot of the plesiosaur's head bobbing through the trees, I assume

**German lobby card for** *Legend of Dinosaurs.* Legend of Dinosaurs and Monster Birds © 1977 Toei.

*One of the new volcano shots in Terremoto 10 Grado.*

*Terremoto 10 Grado's alternate, happy ending.*

*New post-eruption footage.*

*Volcano meant to represent the post eruption Mt. Fuji.*

*End title card which also notes that this was a "Toei Magic Sound System" release.*

for pacing reasons. Then, a shot of the monster bird bobbing its head is shortened as well. Thankfully, the awful attempt at humor where the plesiosaur blinks in bemusement at the Rhamphorynchus as it hops around is cut.

*Terremoto* saves its biggest twist for last. We go through the usual numbers. Mt. Fuji finally erupts for real, and Angie almost falls into a chasm. Aside from the lack of the love ballad, there's nothing too strange about this version until Ashizawa finally manages to grab Angie's hand. This is where all versions of *Legend* end. But not this one. We cut away next to reveal the plesiosaur's fate as it sinks into the ground. OK, I thought, maybe they wanted the last shot to be of the dinosaur?

Footage from the movie's first earthquake (when Ashizawa is exploring Aokigahara) is then integrated into the ending. Notably, in the case of that earthquake, we witness it taper off and end. Then, suddenly Ashizawa and Angie walk out of the cave in a repeated shot from earlier. They survived this movie, whereas their fate is ambiguous at best in *Legend*. Though the footage is the same as earlier, new dialogue is dubbed in for them both stating how, thankfully, the eruption is over.

We pan across some archival footage of a real volcano post eruption with dried lava flows. "Fine" in bright red letters is then superimposed over an aerial shot of an old caldera, and *Terremoto* ends.

All totaled *Terremoto 10 Grado* adds in about eight minutes worth of new footage, though perhaps new isn't entirely correct. I would estimate about five minutes' worth of footage is new to *Legend*, and the other half is repurposed shots from *Legend*, like the ones used to create the new ending.

Unfortunately, today *Terremoto 10 Grado* is a lost film, preserved via VHS thanks to film historians like Max Della Mora. While "Terremoto 10 Grado" did get a DVD release, unfortunately, the Italian DVD doesn't have this version of the film that makes it *Terremoto 10 Grado*. What it has is the Japanese version with the Italian audio spliced back into it best that it can. Whoever edited it must have had a bear of a time doing it too, considering how different the two cuts are. As an added bummer, if you do get the DVD, you won't get to hear any of the rescored scenes either. In all likelihood, the tracks from *The Deep* were probably removed for legal reasons. Though I don't know this for a fact, I would imagine the music was used without permission. The only real vestiges of *Terremoto 10 Grado* from the Italian dub are a few scenes where volcanic eruption noises were added into the background. For instance, you can still hear them in the background of the cabin scene between Ashizawa and "Angie." You can also still hear "King of the Road" during the scene with the two hoaxers. Though there are surely royalties owed on that song too, it managed to slip through the cracks apparently. Though I would like to remain optimistic as to the future of this cut, the odds of it ever being released are slim due to the music rights. The same issue currently plagues the U.S. cut of *The Return of Godzilla*, known as *Godzilla 1985*. For now, your only hope in seeing *Terremoto 10 Grado* is via an old PAL VHS tape. Happy hunting...

## GANBARE! GOJIRA
### OR, GOOD LUCK! GODZILLA

Psst... Wanna see a lost Godzilla movie made by Toho that was shown at events back in 1967? What, you think I'm pulling your leg? Well, I'm not. I might've been just a tad overdramatic, but technically the good news is it really is a "lost Godzilla movie" made by Toho. The bad news is that it's a short film made up of footage from the past five g-films (those being *King Kong vs. Godzilla; Mothra vs. Godzilla; Ghidorah, the Three-Headed Monster; Invasion of Astro-*

Monster; and *Ebirah, Horror of the Deep*).

This short, seven-minute film is a compilation movie that manages to retell *Ghidorah, the Three-Headed Monster* with Ebirah in it, as odd as that sounds. The short was shown for promotional events in 1967 and was included in Toho's Final Box Godzilla set to coincide with *Godzilla: Final Wars*.

The short begins with the Toho logo accompanied by "Night on Bald Mountain" from the classical Russian composer Modest Petrovich Mussorgsky (Toho had a thing for that composition, and it played over the trailers for *Ebirah* and *Conflagration* to name only two times they used it). The title, *Good Luck! Godzilla*, is shown against a white background with red letters as Godzilla roars.

We then cut to Rodan emerging from Mt. Aso from *Ghidorah, the Three-Headed Monster*. Following this is Ghidorah's birth from a meteorite ("Night on Bald Mountain" is still playing, by the way). Just when you think this is an 8mm version of *Ghidorah*, the short throws you a curveball. The next scene is of Ghidorah attacking Japan in *Invasion of Astro-Monster*. Rodan also attacks Japan courtesy of footage from the same film, though it is slightly re-edited. Our next twist comes when Godzilla emerges from an iceberg courtesy of *King Kong vs. Godzilla*. And it gets wilder.

Next thing you know, Ebirah is surfacing from the water to attack a boat. The footage is edited in such a way as to present Godzilla as a hero. Just as Ebirah is about to smash the boat, he's blasted by Godzilla's ray! Before you know it, Godzilla's declawed Ebirah. Suddenly Rodan swoops from the sky and knocks Godzilla over (courtesy the scene of Rodan dive-bombing Godzilla as he emerges from some water in *Ghidorah*).

Rodan picks Godzilla up and then drops him on some high tension wires. The battle continues, but Mothra intervenes, asking the duo to help her battle the space dragon. But Godzilla and Rodan continue the fight, and the edits are interesting. For instance, at one point, the more heavily browed Godzilla from *Mothra vs. Godzilla* gives Rodan a vicious look. So it wasn't simply a matter of condensing footage from *Ghidorah*.

As Rodan soars through the sky, footage of Godzilla chiding Kong is inserted (sans Kong, of course). Then the maser tanks from *Astro-Monster* roll out to more classical music. King Ghidorah descending from the skies to this music is also well done. Mothra crawls into battle with the space dragon, who blasts her away with his gravity beams.

Godzilla enters the fray and the battle is an expertly cut remix that combines *Invasion of Astro-Monster's* final battle with that of *Ghidorah's*. Before we know it, Mothra has webbed up King Ghidorah (Rodan really doesn't help at all in this cut) and the space monster retreats.

Godzilla then helps pull Mothra out of the village with his tail (remember, this scene takes place long before Ghidorah retreats in the real movie). There's a fade that transitions us from Ghidorah in the air to Godzilla jumping off Letchi Island and into the water from *Ebirah, Horror of the Deep*. From that we cut to Mothra swimming away and the "Owari" from *Ghidorah* to close out the film.

A MERIAN C COOPER
PRODUCTION
H RIDER
HAGGARD'S
STOUNDING NOVEL
SHE
WITH
HELEN GAHAGAN
RANDOLPH SCOTT
HELEN MACK
NIGEL BRUCE
AND THOUSANDS OF OTHERS
DIRECTED BY
IRVING PICHEL
LANSING C
HOLDEN

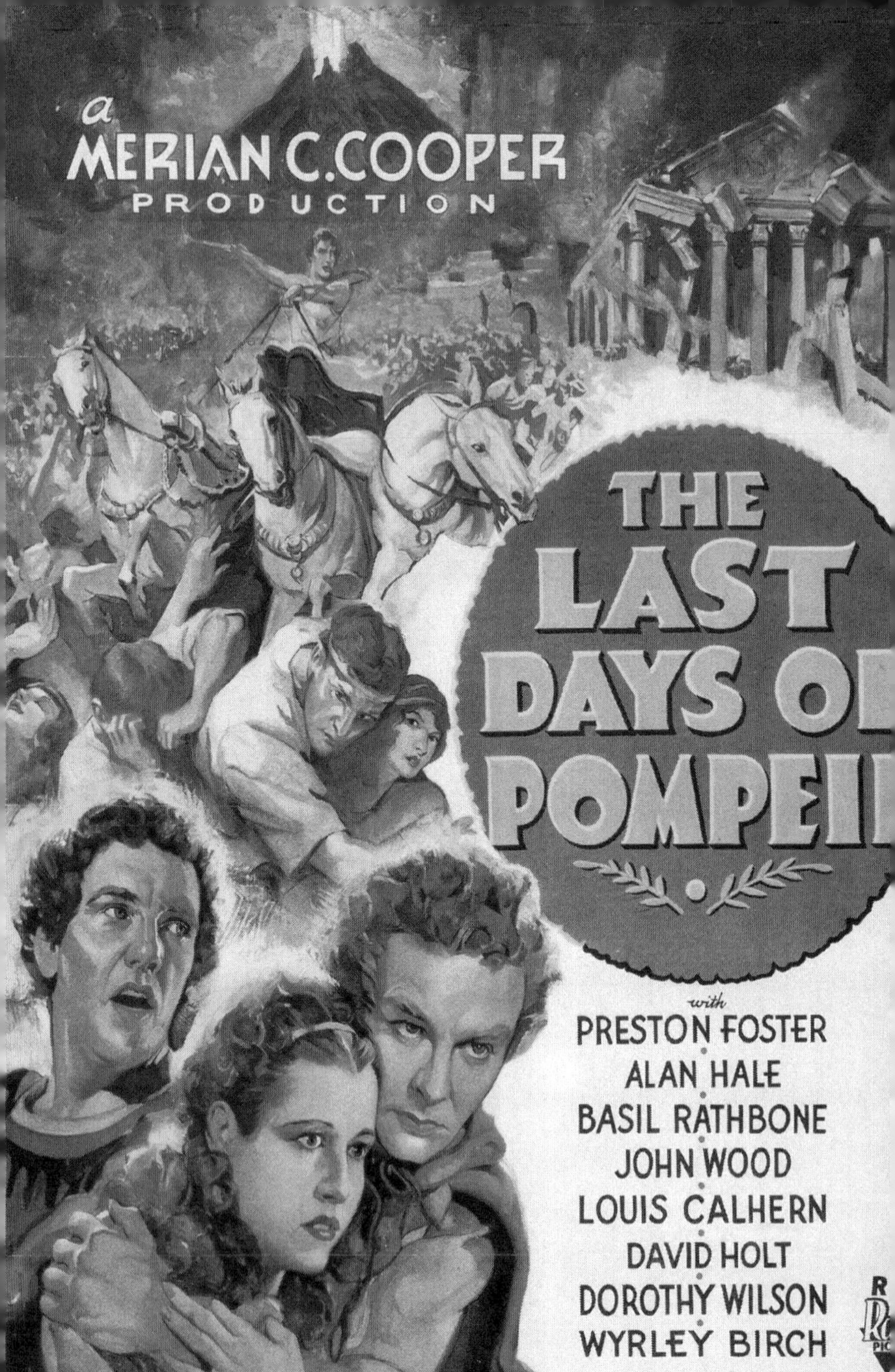
a
MERIAN C. COOPER
PRODUCTION
THE
LAST
DAYS O
POMPEI
with
PRESTON FOSTER
ALAN HALE
BASIL RATHBONE
JOHN WOOD
LOUIS CALHERN
DAVID HOLT
DOROTHY WILSON
WYRLEY BIRCH
DIRECTED BY
ERNEST B. SCHOEDSACK

# "IF IT HAD BEEN IN COLOR WE'D HAVE HAD A BIG HIT!"
## MERIAN C. COOPER'S LOST COLOR EPICS

In 1933, the same year that he unleashed *King Kong* onto the world, Merian C. Cooper encouraged two cousins, John Hay Whitney and Cornelius Vanderbilt Whitney, to begin their own production company called Pioneer Pictures. In late 1934 they hired Cooper to be Pioneer Picture's Vice President with hopes of producing nine full-color features, a rarity in those days. As it was, Technicolor had only been introduced the year before and was mostly limited to Walt Disney cartoons.

Cooper had been dreaming of color pictures as far back as 1932 when he served as head of production at RKO. At that time, Cooper was contemplating a color jungle adventure—NOT *King Kong*, it was already slated for black and white. An inter-office memo related concerns about the "new secret three-color process" and Cooper's idea to construct an artificial jungle set "splashed with brilliant colors..."[1] The untitled jungle adventure, the plot of which is also unknown, would never come to fruition. As it turned out, it would be the first of many disappointments for Cooper when it came to color.

Cooper had hoped that things would be different at Pioneer, where, as stated earlier, nine color films were planned. Among the ambitious titles were *Flying Down to Rio*, *The Three Musketeers*, *The Last Days of Pompeii*, *She*, *Tarzan vs. King Kong*, and *Green Mansions*. Pioneer tested the Technicolor process via the short film, *La Cucaracha*, which ended up winning an Oscar in 1934.

Though some of the planned productions, like *Tarzan vs. King Kong*, didn't materialize, *She* and *The Last Days of Pompeii* would be produced, just not in color. *She* was based upon the novel by H. Rider Haggard, in which explorers find a hidden civilization ruled over by an immortal woman, She Who Must Be Obeyed. Though Cooper changed the setting from Africa to the Arctic, it was basically a faithful adaptation. The same could not be said for the adaptation of Sir Edward Bulwer-Lytton's *Last Days of Pompeii*. The film even acknowledged this with a "foreword" that played after the opening credits which read: "Although ... the characters and plot have no relation to those in the novel by Sir Edward Bulwer-Lytton, acknowledgement is made of his description of Pompeii which has inspired the physical setting of this picture."[2] That all said, the story was, of course, based upon the real-life eruption of Mount Vesuvius in A.D.79, which decimated the town of Pompeii.

It was hoped that these two productions, filmed in 1934, would top the spectacle of King Kong. As it was, much of the same crew were working on the two films. Ruth Rose wrote both, Willis O'Brien was to help with the effects on both, and Ernest B. Schoedsack would direct Pompeii. Ultimately neither film would live up to Kong. Film costs had risen drastically since 1933, and RKO (who had a stake in Pioneer Pictures) cut both film's budgets in half. Initially, both were slated to cost $1 million each, now Cooper would have to produce both of them for $1 million total. This nixed the color photography. Also, RKO didn't inform Cooper of the cut until after extensive pre-production work had been done for She. Cooper initially wanted to cut She all together, and funnel all $1 million into Pompeii, but RKO wanted both pictures and wouldn't allow it. Cooper had to compensate, and as he put it, "I cheated a lot on She."[3]

A loss of color wasn't the only thing that affected the productions, monstrous animals not dissimilar to Kong were scripted for each production as well. Though the explorers do find a frozen saber-toothed tiger in She,[4] it never comes to life, and Cooper had wanted O'Brien to animate a herd of mammoths for the film. Said mammoths would attack the explorers. For Last Days of Pompeii, the animals would aid rather than attack the characters. As an arena

This is a rare test shot of one of the dinosaurs from *Son of Kong* shot in color c.1934 by Pioneer Pictures, perhaps as a test for *Tarzan vs. King Kong*?

**Colorized lobby card for *Last Days of Pompeii* (left) and colorized film frame from *She* (right).**

floods with water, Obie envisioned men hopping onto giant swordfish and riding them out of the arena!!! But, as with the mammoths, giant swordfish were not an additional cost that the production could handle.

Though Cooper had promised RKO executives that *Pompeii's* climactic eruption would rival the ending of *King Kong*, audiences didn't agree, and *Pompeii* lost over $200,000 at the box office when all was said and done. Neither was *She* a big hit.

Cooper seemed to mourn *Pompeii* more so than *She*, which he considered the worst picture he ever did. *Pompeii*, on the other hand, might have held sentimental value for him as he had toured the real Pompeii during his honeymoon and envisioned a film adaptation in color on the spot. In later years he lamented, "If it had been in color we'd have had a big hit!"[5]

There's still a silver lining to the two films, though. When re-released on a double bill in 1949 they were actually hits, and both finally managed to turn a profit for RKO. Furthermore, in tribute to Cooper, Ray Harryhausen and Legend Films saw to it that *She* was colorized in 2006. Maybe one day someone will take it upon themselves to do the same for *The Last Days of Pompeii*?

---

[1] Cotta Vaz, Mark, *Living Dangerously: The Adventures of Merian C. Cooper*, pp.265.
[2] Let us not forget that Cooper bought the rights to remake *The Lost World* when working on *King Kong*.
[3] *Living Dangerously*, pp. 261.
[4] This all came about when Ruth Rose quipped that *She* had everything in it but a saber-toothed tiger and Cooper told her to write one in!
[5] *Living Dangerously*, pp.263.

# OUR NEXT

MUSIC LAXMIKANT PYARELAL PRODUCED BY PREM LALWANI AND MOHAN LALWA

# AATANK ATTACKS!
## BOLLYWOOD'S LOST SHARK MOVIE

Do you like the Jaws series, but hate the current deluge of crappy CGI shark movies? Good, me too. Do you also love early 1970s era tokusatsu TV effects... let's say, *Spectreman*, for example? Me too! Well, if you like *Jaws*, hate CGI sharks, and love old tokusatsu, then you might like parts of *Aatank*.

I was first introduced to *Aatank* through my friend Lee Powers, who posted a picture of what appeared to be a Megalodon toy bearing down on a little toy man. Over time I learned the still belonged to a Bollywood movie called *Aatank*. And, as it turned out, the shark was not a Megalodon. It was a normal Great White that the Bollywood SPFX technicians had accidentally made an error in scale with. That occurs throughout the whole movie, by the way. Sometimes the shark is about the size of Bruce in *Jaws*, while other times, it's almost kaiju-sized.

Eventually, I found a clip of the film on YouTube. Though the effects looked like they were from the late 1960s, I knew the effects had to be at least ten years older than this as this was clearly a *Jaws* rip-off. Further confusing the matter was that this movie's release date was given as 1996 when all the footage was obviously shot in the late 1970s or early 1980s!

Finally, I discovered the truth. *Aatank* began shooting in the early 1980s (though some sources have claimed that it shot in the late 1970s). Like *Grizzly II: Revenge*, a great deal of footage had been shot before production shut down. As to why the film was shut down, that I do not know.

What I do know is that in 1990, *Aatank's* completed footage came up for auction and was purchased by Bemisaal Productions. It's unknown if Bemisaal Productions simply planned to edit together the existing footage, or if they had ideas of filming additional footage.

Whatever the case, the movie's lead actor, Dharmendra, saw Bemisaal's rough cut and volunteered his services to help finish the movie. Lucky for Bemisaal

31/THE LOST FILMS FANZINE #1

Productions, Dharmendra had become a superstar since the 1980s.

As funny as this sounds, Dharmendra actually shot additional scenes for the movie to fill in the story blanks, though he is noticeably older! The other missing scenes were trickier, as the actors who had played those parts had passed on. Therefore body doubles were used to complete certain scenes, while in other cases, new characters altogether were created to fill in the blanks.

When finally released in 1996, it only grossed ₹6,900,000 on a ₹15,000,000 budget. This isn't necessarily surprising considering the quality of the shark effects either, which were behind the times to begin with.

If anything, the huge shark looks like a giant bathtub toy. A bathtub toy that tears people to shreds, that is. Though scary in spite of the bad effects, I would have to compare these scenes to the killings in *Legend of Dinosaurs and Monster Birds*. Overall, there's an odd juxtaposition between the fake-looking monster prop and the exploitive amount of gore from the attacks. Furthermore, every time we see the shark approaching, we hear a tiger's roar!

If you're into bad effects, then *Aatank* is definitely a movie you'll want to see, but be warned, the shark doesn't show until almost an hour in. Plus, this is a Bollywood movie, which means that it's fairly long, has lots of dance numbers, and is essentially a soap opera.

Within the story's first ten minutes the main character, an orphan boy named Jesu, is whipped by a priest, his best friend Peter falls into a well, Jesu then gets adopted by Peter's mother, and in the next scene, the woman is on her death bed! The sequence then concludes with the boys being separated, and we then jump into the future where both are now adults.

*Director*: Prem Lalwani & Desh Mukherjee *Script*: Sachin Bhowmick *Special Effects*: Sanjay Naik *Music*: Laxmikant Shantaram Kudalkar (as Laxmikant), Rameshwer Pyarelal, Ramprasad Sharma (as Pyarelal) & Kamal Singh *Cast*: Jesu (Dharmendra), Peter (Vinod Mehra), Jesu's girlfriend (Hema Malini), Inspector Khan (Girish Karnad) *Release Date*: 1996 *Runtime*: 113 Minutes familiar?). The ending takes no prisoners. As the soap opera drama continues, Jesu's adopted son and a friend take to the waters on a sailboat at the same time that Jesu is hunting the shark. Naturally, the monster shark comes along and eats the friend in what is probably the movie's best remembered scene. Jesu's son manages to survive, though (the movie's not that cruel).

The badly disconnected subplot about the evil tycoon whose been wronging the villagers for the past two hours is also resolved when the shark eats him. Specifically, while the bad guy is escaping on a boat, a helicopter comes to his rescue. In a crude attempt to top the helicopter scene from *Jaws 2*, the shark jumps out of the water and smashes the chopper! The explosion catapults the villain through the air, and with precision aim, Jesu throws a harpoon through him!

In adulthood, the two adopted brothers reside in the same fishing village, which lives in fear of an evil mob boss who controls the shores. At the same time, a gigantic shark appears and begins killing the villagers. It will be up to Jesu to do away with both the shark, and the mob boss...

The shark makes its grand entrance in the middle of a Bollywood dance number. Its debut is similar to the shark in *Jaws*, if Chrissy Watkins was singing a big musical number in the water! The woman is Peter's wife, who is singing to him from the ocean while Peter is too drunk to follow her in. The shark pops up unexpectedly in the middle of the song to swallow the woman whole! And what a big shark it is (easily bigger than the one in *Jaws*). Later, while Jesu and Peter are out to avenge Peter's wife, the shark eats Peter! Jesu must then avenge Peter, and this plot point then drives the rest of the movie... mostly.

The story's climax consists of Jesu and the Chief of Police going out on a small boat to kill the shark (sound

Then it's time for he-man Jesu to deal with the shark. For some reason it jumps over Jesu's boat, and when it does, Jesu digs a harpoon into its stomach. It gets stuck, and so Jesu gets dragged into the water with the massive shark.

The dead shark, a life-size prop, washes up on the beach with Jesu, who survives, by the way, clinging to it. As the excited villagers rush to the shark the movie ends.

If you wish to see this Bollywood musical version of *Jaws* it is currently out there waiting to be discovered in the depths of the internet...

33/THE LOST FILMS FANZINE #1

# IMITATION SPAGHETTI

**Strange Adventures of Coby and Ben; My Name is Trinity** Ital. *Director:* Ferdinando Baldi *Script:* Ferdinando Baldi, Nico Ducci & Mino Roli *Camera:* Aiace Parolin *Music:* Franco Bixio & Vince Tempera *Cast:* Michael Coby (Coby) Paul L. Smith (Clem Rodovam) William Bogart ("Kelly for 50") Horst Frank (Clydeson) Pino Ferrara (Sheriff) Melissa Chimenti (Pamela) *Release Date:* September 13, 1974 *Runtime:* 96 Minutes

## MY NAME IS TRINITY AND TRINITY AND CARAMBOLA

First of all, my title for this article is a bit off. It should be "Imitation Beans," because there's a difference between a Spaghetti Western and a "Beans Western" (even though they both still come from Italy).

A Spaghetti Western signified a straight western made in Italy, while a Beans Western was a comedy western or spoof of sorts. By 1970 the Spaghetti Western had reached its zenith. The market was oversaturated, and audiences were getting tired of the same ol' same ol'. And then came along a little film called *They Call Me Trinity* (1970). It starred Terence Hill and Bud Spencer as a couple of estranged, head cracking brothers Trinity and Bambino. Trinity was the handsome swindler played by Hill, while Bambino was the big, burly brute. Though the duo are outlaws, they end up saving a group of Mormon settlers from an evil land baron. The film was a hit, followed by an even more successful sequel: *Trinity is Still My Name* (1971). And, because both films have significant sequences of the brothers scarfing down helpings of beans, henceforth comedic Italian westerns were called Beans Westerns.

Both Trinity films broke records as the highest grossing Italian films of their time. So just chew on that

34/THE LOST FILMS FANZINE #1

for a minute. Even though most Westerners know all about Sergio Leone's Dollars trilogy, which concluded with *The Good, the Bad, and the Ugly*, it was out-grossed by a comedy spoof. And yet, by comparison, few Americans know of the Trinity films when compared to Leone's.

And, considering most Americans don't know who Hill and Spencer are, they damn sure won't know who Paul Coby and Michael Smith are. Just as Dean Martin and Jerry Lewis had their look-a-like imitators, Sonny Petrillo and Duke Mitchell, Hill and Spencer had Coby and Smith. Both men looked remarkably like Hill and Spencer and were put together intentionally by Italian producer Manolo Bolognini. His intent was naturally to trick audiences into thinking that the duo were Hill and Spencer, though he never went so far as to actually try and pass them off as such.

You see, even though Hill and Spencer continued to work together, they never did do a third Trinity movie (although, director Enzo Barboni has said he mused one called "And They Insist Upon Calling Him Trinity"). Even though audiences could still see Hill and Spencer on-screen, their new movies were often contemporary affairs where the duo played cops, conmen, missionaries, race car drivers, you name it, but no more westerns together.

Producer Bolognini wanted to sate audiences' demand for another Trinity-type movie with Hill and Spencer, so he gave them the next best thing in the form of lookalikes Coby and Smith in 1974's *Carambola* (called *My Name is Trinity* in some places). Though Bolognini didn't go so far as to name the characters Trinity and Bambino—and he could have considering how many Djangos ran around Italy—Coby is dressed exactly like Hill's Trinity and the same went for Smith. The movie's first and last scene even shares the same set-ups as the Trinity sequel.

35/THE LOST FILMS FANZINE #1

**Lobby card for *Carambola* AKA *My Name is Trinity*. Smith is on the left and Coby on the right.**

*Carambola* begins in the same sandy, white desert as *Trinity is Still My Name* and ends at a river crossing, which is also how the Trinity sequel ends. Therefore one really could consider this a poor man's "Trinity 3."

The story concerns a pool hustler, Coby, who is caught with a deadly, prototype handgun. The army then tasks him with tracking down the gun's maker to avoid prison time. Coby insists upon the help of his friend/enemy Clem, a ne'er do well strongman. This was meant to parallel Trinity and Bambino, who, despite being brothers, despised each other.

To enlist Clem, Coby has him arrested under false charges and the duo then stage a fake jailbreak together (which is absolutely something Trinity would do to Bambino). Near the border of Mexico, the duo finds the maker of the gun and forces him to sign a confession during a train robbery that they stage. In the end, the U.S. army can't pay Coby and Clem what they owe them due to all the property damage the duo caused!

Ultimately, despite the resemblance, Coby and Smith are no Hill and Spencer. The movie's shortcomings probably lie more so in the direction than Coby and Smith, though. Had *Trinity* director Enzo Barboni helmed the film things may have been different because certain scenes have potential. There's a great trick pool sequence early in the film, for instance, that would fit right in with the Trinity series (considering that Trinity was a card shark in the second film, doing trick shots with pool would seem to be the next natural progression had the series went on). Another great scene worthy of Bambino occurs when Smith's horse tires out, and so his character Clem dismounts and begins to carry the horse on his shoulders! (Like Bambino, Clem is a lover of horses). The scene is also often mistaken for a scene from the Trinity films, actually.

Clem, still carrying the horse, comes upon a stagecoach and remarks, "My horse has a hangnail and I'm tired of carrying him!" Later, the film outright copies a scene from *My Name is Nobody* (another Hill vehicle) where Coby slaps a man multiple times before he can draw his gun.

As for scenes with potential that fell short, the duo comes across a karate school at one point. It's amusing enough, but Hill, Spencer, and Barboni probably could have worked wonders with the same scenario. Similarly, the film caps off with an amusing train hold-up, something else Trinity and Bambino never did but probably could have done better.

I don't know what the box office numbers for *Carambola* were, but it apparently did well enough to spawn *Carambola's Philosophy: In the Right Pocket* in 1975.

This one begins in a ghost town, where Coby and Clem witness the cavalry testing out a top-secret new weapon: a motorcycle with a Gatling gun in the sidecar. The duo steals the motorcycle and is pursued by the cavalry and an outlaw who wants the cycle himself. A merry chase full of wanton destruction occurs in a town where the cycle crashes.

Afterward, Coby and Clem are forced to work off their debt. In the end, Coby is arrested by the cavalry, and Clem impersonates a general to rescue him. The duo then speeds off in the cycle once again, with the cavalry and the entire town on their tail.

This direct in-continuity sequel to *Carambola* was produced by the same exact crew as before. Arguably, the sequel is funnier than the original. It's not too different from the plot structure of *Trinity is Still My Name* in that there isn't much of a plot, just a series of comedic set pieces strung together. The motorcycle with the Gatling gun, for instance, is simply a tedious thread to hold it all together and appears only at the beginning and the end.

The sequel's first scenes are promising. Coby promises to take Clem to "a town that's got it all" which turns out to be a festering pit of despair not unlike the town in *Keoma* (1976). All in all, it's a fairly good attempt to spoof the ghost town angle used in some of the

*Trinity and Carambola; The Crazy Adventures of Len and Coby* Ital. *Director:* Ferdinando Baldi *Script:* Ferdinando Baldi, Nico Ducci & Mino Roli *Camera:* Aiace Parolin *Music:* Franco Bixio & Vince Tempera *Producer:* Manolo Bolognini *Cast:* Michael Coby (Coby) Paul L. Smith (Clem Rodovam) Glauco Onorato (El Supremo) Ray O'Connor (El Supremo lieutenant) Gabriella Andreini (Miss Peabody) Pino Ferrara (Sheriff) Piero Lulli (Colonel) Enzo Monteduro (coffin maker) Benjamin Lev (Deputy sheriff) *Release Date:* February 22, 1975 *Runtime:* 70 Minutes

*German lobby card featuring the duo riding the motorcycle that drives the plot.*

odder spaghettis like *Matalo* (1970). Later, there's a scene where the villain holds up a stagecoach, and due to the dialogue between he and the stagecoach driver, it's clear that this is a normal routine. This scene, in particular, is evocative of the style of the Trinity films and Barboni's *Man of the East*.

The best sequence is the ending. Coby and Clem have stolen the cycle for a second time, and now the military cavalry and the entire town are chasing them down. The duo is going too fast and plunge off a cliff and into a river. The pursuers all stop atop the precipice to mourn their passing in humorous ways. "Now who am I going to arrest?" laments the sheriff. The undertaker tearfully remarks, "I never even got to measure them for caskets." Cut to Coby and Clem rowing downstream in a boat. "I bet this takes us all the way to the Pacific," Coby says. "Where's that? I thought this was taking us to the ocean," says Clem. The excited duo is certain that they can hear the noisy ocean waves. The camera pans over a ways to reveal the two are heading for a gargantuan waterfall! The shot freeze frames, and the credits roll.

Amusing as the two films are, all they really do is make one pine for a real third Trinity movie. It also makes one wonder what Enzo Barboni's direction might have done with the scenarios presented within the two films.

Like the twin Trinity movies, this was Coby and Smith's last turns as Coby and Clem. Ultimately it was the second of what would be five pictures together for the duo, who, like Spencer and Hill, would make pictures in contemporary settings next.

# THE LOST SEQUEL OF DR. PHIBES

Considering that only two films consist of the Dr. Phibes franchise, those being *The Abominable Dr. Phibes* (1971) and *Dr. Phibes Rises Again* (1972), there exists a surprising number of unmade Phibes films. There were, naturally, the first cracks at the Phibes story that differed from the debut film, and then there were the numerous drafts for the first sequel (*Dr. Phibes vs. Count Yorga* anyone?). Most of the unmade ideas, treatments, and scripts focused on an unproduced third film. In addition to this, there was even talk of Phibes popping up in other movies, such as the time he almost teamed with Fu Manchu to battle James Bond and Inspector Clouseau in an aborted version of *The Pink Panther Strikes Again*! There have also been a few remakes pitched, such as one from Tim Burton to star Johnny Depp, which never came to be.

So, as you can see, there are plenty of projects to discuss, but this issue we are going to cover *The Brides of Dr. Phibes*—initially a sequel to the first film, which, when rejected in favor of *Rises Again*, was then pitched as the third film in the series. So it has an interesting track record.

*The Abominable Dr. Phibes* was set in the 1920s and focused on a macabre musician, Dr. Anton Phibes, who was horribly burned in a car crash (therefore, he wears prosthetics to hide his deformities). The accident occurred because Phibes was racing home upon the news of his wife Victoria's death. The embittered Phibes believes his wife died due to carelessness on the part of the surgeons, so he plots to kill each of them in wildly inventive ways. The film ends with Phibes killing all but one of the doctors (in the case of the last surgeon, Phibes planned to kill the man's son, but fails in his endeavor). In the final scene, the mad doctor evades authorities by putting he and his

39/THE LOST FILMS FANZINE #1

preserved wife into a state of suspended animation within a hidden tomb. The film was a hit, and so AIP commissioned writers William Goldstein and James Whiton to script a sequel right away.

In tribute to *Bride of Frankenstein*, they called the story *The Bride of Dr. Phibes*. It had Phibes awaken ten years later, in 1934, only to find the body of his beloved Victoria gone. Phibes, who believes that he can still resurrect Victoria through medical advancements, sets out to find just who took the body. To aid in his quest, Phibes tracks down his assistant, Vulnavia, who survived the first film but was scarred with acid and placed within a mental institution. Phibes rescues her and performs facial reconstruction surgery on her (Vulnavia was always meant as eye candy for the male members of the audience).

On the trail of Victoria, Phibes eventually finds that she was taken by the members of an occult society belonging to the Institute of Psychic Phenomena. Phibes begins to dispatch its members in unique ways. Whereas the first film had Phibes recreating the Biblical plagues of Exodus, in this script, there's no real theme to Phibes' killings. One man finds a nest of cobras in his bed, another is drained of all blood by leeches in a spa, and another is eviscerated by way of vacuum cleaner. One man is even carried away by balloon.

As the story progresses, Phibes finds out who his enemy really is: Lem Vesalius, the son of the doctor whom Phibes tried to kill ten years previous. Despite being a sympathetic innocent in the first film, Vesalius Jr. is now an outright villain, though his motives are understandable. In a final showdown, Phibes defeats his nemesis inside of Vesalius's at-home slaughterhouse.

But it's not over yet. Victoria's heart has been surgically removed and given to another returning character from the first film: Inspector Trout. The inspector has set a trap for Phibes, telling him to meet him at Wimbley Stadium if he wants his wife's heart back. Phibes outsmarts Trout by constructing a clockwork decoy of himself to walk into the stadium, while Phibes himself is disguised as a policeman. Phibes gets the heart while Trout and the others are distracted, and then drives off in a police car!

The last scenes are a rehash of the first movie, where Vulnavia holds off the police while Phibes makes final preparations on Victoria. In this case, Vulnavia fends off the police with a bow and arrow and then commits suicide! (Guess they didn't care if Vulnavia came back for Phibes #3?) Phibes successfully revives Victoria and then places the duo into yet another state of suspended animation before the police can find them.

AIP rejected this script, and I have to say I'm happy that they did, as I think Dr. Phibes' trip to Egypt in the sequel was spectacular. Speaking of *Dr. Phibes Rises Again*, it underperformed to the extent that there wasn't a great deal of enthusiasm for a third film. (During shooting, ideas for a third movie were discussed by director Robert Fuest, which included an untitled story where Phibes would battle Nazis in the 1930s, and a different concept called *Son of Dr. Phibes*.)

The chronology of the aborted third Phibes film is difficult to pin down exactly, but *Castle of Frankenstein* #20 (c.1974) reported that: "A second 'Phibes' sequel has been announced: THE BRIDES OF DOCTOR PHIBES." What had happened was, when AIP showed their disinterest for another Phibes, writers Goldstein and Whiton revised their *Bride* script (possibly to infer that it now takes place after *Rises Again,* but this isn't certain) and then took it to Roger Corman at his New World Pictures. Corman was interested and thought about shooting the movie for a 1977 release.

With Phibes, Victoria, and Vulnavia having set sail on the mystic River of Life at the end of *Rises Again,* the original opening of *Bride* would have to be revised to reflect this.

In Bride #2, Phibes makes a grand entrance in a hot air balloon. According to the book *The Price of Fear: The Film Career of Vincent Price, In His Own Words,* Phibes would go to retrieve Victoria from a crypt. How she got to the tomb from the River of Life is curious, so perhaps Whiton and Goldstein were actually pulling a retcon of *Rises Again*? (Though, if this was the case, then why wouldn't they simply awaken from their crypts as they do in *Rises Again*?)

In any case, the story follows the same outline as before with minor differences, such as Phibes riding a motorcycle (rather than taking his car) to rescue Vulnavia, once again in a mental institution. (Considering this, it's becoming more and more likely that *Bride* was one of those sequels that ignored the last film à la *Jaws The Revenge* and *Jaws 3*.)

The death by cobras scene was replaced by having the same victim dipped in a vat of chlorine. The vacuum cleaner scene was made more graphic, with a man getting inflated like a balloon and then deflating so hard he flies through the air!

Bride #2 ends the same as #1, only now Vulnavia is dressed as a Native American as she fires bows and arrows at the police. She is aided along by mechanical, clockwork cowboys constructed by Phibes. And, this time, Vulnavia lives. Phibes puts himself and Victoria into a deep freeze. When the police fail to find them, the following message flashes across a scoreboard: "I SHALL RETURN!" The song "New York, New York" was then to begin playing, hinting at the next story's locale.

The project moved along at New World with casting discussions. Oddly enough, it is said that David Carradine was eyed for Phibes! However, I wonder if Carradine was eyed for a different attempt to film *Bride* in the 1980s, but I'm getting ahead of myself.

Among the cast eyed for the 1977 *Bride of Dr. Phibes*, now retitled *Phibes Resurrectus*, were Paul Williams as Lem Vesalius, Orson Wells as a psychic named Dr. Steuben, and Roddy McDowall as Vicar Wren. Also among the proposed cast was Coral Browne, Vincent Price's wife! The casting of Browne has led many to believe that Price was going to return as Phibes. Further evidence of this is the fact that *Famous Monsters* editor Forry Ackerman was going to play the mechanical Phibes decoy, as there was a long running joke about Forry resembling Vincent Price. Justin Humphries, author of *The Dr. Phibes Companion*, puts forth a clever theory that perhaps Roger Corman mentioned casting Carradine as Phibes as a way of scaring Price into lowering his fee.

For reasons unknown, *Phibes Resurrectus* went quietly into the night at New World. Perhaps feeling the script wasn't up to snuff, Whiton and Goldstein then offered an alternate Phibes 3, which again ignored *Rises Again*. It was called

41/THE LOST FILMS FANZINE #1

**The good doctor at his pipe organ.** © 1971 The Abominable Dr. Phibes.

*Phibes in the Holy Land* and had Phibes at war with a fellow composer! That idea, too, was dropped in favor of revamping *Bride of Dr. Phibes* again.

This attempt was bandied about in the early 1980s and called *Dr. Phibes*. The doctor, Victoria, and Vulnavia arrive in New York, where Phibes hopes American medicine can help him revive his wife. Phibes and co. hole up in a New York penthouse, and soon find themselves at war with the Wormwood Institute. Rather than occultists, this organization is made up of sinister scientists, one of whom dabbles in germ warfare. Their leader, Hector Wormwood (this story's stand-in for Lem Vesalius), breaks Victoria's crystal casket, causing her to shrivel up and decompose. It's then a race against time for Phibes to find the essential salts to restore her and kill all the members of the Wormwood Society along the way.

The story was said to get as far along as a treatment, but not a full-blown script. In 1984, Laurel Entertainment announced *Phibes Resurrectus* among its slated projects, and presumably, it was based upon this treatment (though no one knows for sure).

To this day, William Goldstein is still trying to get more Phibes projects off the ground, the most recent effort being *Phibes Forever*. That one was supposed to have been out in 2016 and star Malcolm McDowell as Phibes.

For those hungry for official Phibes content, it should be noted that Goldstein authored a prequel novel, *Dr. Phibes—In the Beginning*, and also a Vulnavia spin-off, *Vulnavia's Secret*, that features the escape from the mental institute from *Bride/Resurrectus*.

# The Top 10 Godzilla Fan Trailers

Godzilla fans have been splicing together their own unique Godzilla trailers and mini-movies since the days of Super 8mm film. However, the digital age has opened up a multitude of new possibilities when it comes to digital editing—especially in terms of fan-made trailers. With the right tools, a regular fan like you or I can overlay new text across the screen, re-edit the audio to add or remove music/sound fx, or just edit existing footage together in unique ways. What we're about to discuss here are the best of the best fan-made Godzilla trailers. Some are made up concepts entirely (like *Godzilla Appears in Edo*), while others are based on real-life cancelled projects like *Frankenstein vs. Godzilla*.

**Godzilla vs. Dracula** Honorable Mention
This mashup between the trailers for Lugosi's 1933 *Dracula* and *Godzilla, King of the Monsters* (1956) is very well done from an editorial perspective. However, the trains never quite meet, so to speak, and it's unclear how Godzilla and Dracula might cross paths. This trailer really is essentially a very skilled combination of the previews for *Dracula* and the U.S. version of *Godzilla*. Sometimes Godzilla's theme is played over sequences of Dracula and vice versa. Again, though it's unclear how these two monsters are going to meet, it's very well edited, and the creator did the best they could with the limited source material. If anything, I would believe that it was a trailer for a double bill for *Godzilla* and *Dracula*.

#10. Kenny Wars
You've heard of *Final Wars*, but how about *Kenny Wars*? There may be no monsters in this trailer, but hey, laughs score you points too! Thanks to *MST3K* by way of Sandy Frank's Gamera releases, the term "Kenny" has become synonymous with the child characters in Japanese monster movies. This particular trailer, by Space Hunter M, has the various Kenny's (notably Ichiro from *All Monster's Attack*, Koh from *6 Ultra Brothers vs. the Monster Army*, Roku-san from *Godzilla vs. Megalon*, plus all the Gamera brats) fighting it out amongst one another. And it doesn't mess around.

With *Godzilla vs. Biollante* composer Koichi Sugiyama's "Bio Wars" rock-track blasting, we see a shot of Christopher Murphy's Tom character from *Gamera vs. Guiron* firing off his dart gun. The "bullet" then hits Koh from *6 Ultra Brothers* in a bloody headshot! (In the movie Koh is shot semi-graphically in the

43/THE LOST FILMS FANZINE #1

Christopher Murphy is on the loose!

And it's Masaaki Daimon who pays the price!

Ichiro charges at Gabara!

Title card for "Kenny Wars".

Coming Soon! If only...

The title card for "Godzilla vs. Gamera" superimposed over a shot of *Gamera vs. Barugon*.

head by thieves. Hey, Thai kid's movies have different standards!). The title "Kenny Wars" is then superimposed over Murphy's bicycle spokes, and it's hilarious.

"'GANG FIGHTING!" the trailer proclaims as Ichiro knocks over Gabara in *All Monsters Attack*. More scenes of Kenny tantrums follow, like Eiichi throwing his toys off the porch in *Gamera vs. Gyaos*, then Ichiro throwing trash at the bank robber as the trailer proclaims "VIOLENCE AND DELINQUENCY!"

"MERCILESS KILLINGS" flashes over the screen as Murphy points his dart gun again, and this time Masaaki Daimon is riddled with bullets in slow motion via *Terror of Mechagodzilla*. The trailer goes on with an excellent action cut of all the various Kenny's in action until "Bio Wars" begins to trail off. Bravo, Space Hunter M, bravo!

#9. Godzilla vs. Gamera 1980
Although there are plenty of "Godzilla vs. Gamera" trailers to pick from, this one is my favorite. This one kicks off with a volcanic eruption courtesy of 1973's *Submersion of Japan*, which essentially serves as the backbone of the whole trailer. Dr. Tadokoro, a character from that film, looks through a porthole and spies Gamera making his entrance on a beach (courtesy *Gamera vs. Viras*). Gamera roars, then we cut to a close-up of an angry Godzilla from *Terror of Mechagodzilla*. The trailer title, "Godzilla vs. Gamera", is then superimposed across a longshot of Barugon destroying Kobe from *Gamera vs. Barugon*. It's a fantastic start through and through.

This is followed by some more dramatic footage from *Submersion* giving the trailer an epic feel. Following this is well-edited footage of Gyaos, Godzilla, and

44/THE LOST FILMS FANZINE #1

Gamera all on the loose with a few quality FX shots from *Submersion's* Kanto earthquake thrown in for good measure. Godzilla then appears to observe Gamera landing in the city and a short battle takes place that, aside from a few audio issues, is good visually speaking.

Later, it is made to appear as though Gyaos has caused a tidal wave from *Submersion*! The trailer teases one more battle clip between the titular titans, with Gamera throwing a rock in *Viras* that hits Godzilla in the knee courtesy of *Zone Fighter*. Though I'm not exactly sure what the story was supposed to be, the basics come across: monsters are loose, Japan is being destroyed, and Godzilla and Gamera are gonna fight!

#8. Godzilla and the Deadly Four

The only reason this trailer doesn't rank higher is because of its brevity. (Not that brevity is a bad thing, I just want to acknowledge the trailers that took more time to edit.)

The trailer gets its idea across easily: Samurai assassins have been hired to kill Godzilla. The creator, Scott David Lister, writes, "Godzilla meets his match against Lone Wolf and Cub's Itto Ogami, Jimmy Wang Yu's One-Armed Swordsman, the blind but dangerous masseur Zatoichi, and Toshiro Mifune's crafty Yojimbo. With all of the bloodletting and violence you'd come to expect from a 1970's chanbara flick!"

And, even if they wouldn't stand a chance in Godzilla's world, in whatever alternate fantasy reality this story takes place in, it seems believable. There are well-edited cuts that make it appear as though the Deadly Four each cut Godzilla with their swords (courtesy the bloodier scenes from the 70's era films). The music is also well plac-

**Gamera makes his entrance into the trailer.**

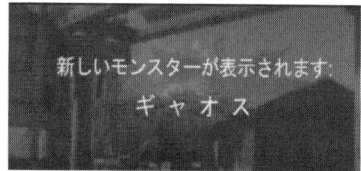

**"A new monster" the trailer proclaims over this shot of Gyaos.**

**Destruction shots were mostly from *Submersion of Japan* (1973).**

**Godzilla after Gamera's just hit him with a rock.**

**One of the first frames of *Godzilla and the Deadly Four*.**

**One of the deadly four.**

**Godzilla's been cut!**

45/THE LOST FILMS FANZINE #1

*Godzilla roars a challenge to...*

*Daiei's Daimajin!*

*Godzilla comes ashore via an unused outtake on the Son of Godzilla trailer.*

*The Red Bamboo learns of Godzilla's arrival.*

*The Big G roars a challenge...*

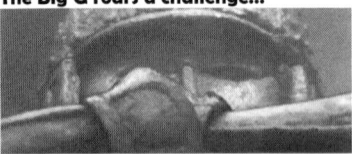

*As Daimajin begins his transformation.*

*Daimajin walks through the lake.*

*Final frame of the trailer.*

-ed. The trailer, aside from the wild concept, seems totally believable.

For bonus points, this trailer ends with a teaser for *Godzilla vs. Redmoon*!

#7. Godzilla vs. Daimajin
The trailer begins with a shot of Godzilla from the *Godzilla vs. Megalon* trailer, followed by a shot of Daimajin from one of his trailers set to Godzilla's theme. A fireball strikes the water in a dynamic shot, and from here the narrative is easy to follow.

Godzilla emerges from the ocean (from *Son of Godzilla*) and begins walking through the jungle, trampling what is, in reality, the Red Bamboo Base from *Ebirah*. The chaos extends underground, all the way to a hidden Daimajin statue (*Return of Daimajin*). The Daimajin then emerges from the water (also from *Return*). There are various edits that make it appear as though the monsters are about to face off— but, a good trailer never gives too much away, so we don't actually see them fight (that, and it's impossible).

One of the better edits has Majin bursting through a building followed by Godzilla's head rising out of the water from *Godzilla vs. Mechagodzilla* (1974). As Godzilla walks, the Red Bamboo takes note of him and begins an attack, and the music changes to one of Ifukube's battle themes.

In another good tease, Godzilla roars against a stormy night sky (footage from *Ebirah*) while Majin transforms from stone into monster against a similar stormy sky, making it appear as though they are in the same place at the same time. This trailer presents an excellent edit all around!

#6. Godzilla vs. Frankenstein
"From the fiery depths of Earth comes a prehistoric mastodon of destruction!" proclaims the trailer, which originally, of course, referred to Baragon. But here it works too because Godzilla emerges from the earth courtesy of footage from the *Godzilla vs. the Thing* trailer.

That's what this preview essentially is: a very well done combo of the U.S. trailers for *Thing* and *Frankenstein Conquers the World*. The audio from the FCTW trailer is used very well. Unfortunately, the voice actor never did a Godzilla trailer, meaning the creator of the new trailer couldn't scavenge an audio bite from one because none ever existed. If it did, it would have made this trailer 100% believable. My only teeny tiny beef with it is that it included a shot of Mothra's egg that I felt should have been removed. Otherwise, it's excellent. There's even a great shot of Godzilla hitting Frankenstein with his atomic ray...even if it does change color from blue to orange.

This one was based on a real concept that was seriously considered by Toho in 1964 as a follow-up to *Mothra vs. Godzilla* (renamed *Godzilla vs. the Thing* by AIP). Instead, Baragon was created to replace Godzilla and *Frankenstein Conquers the World* was released in 1965. Unfortunately, this is one of the few trailers on this list that's been taken down from YouTube (at least, I couldn't find it this time around).

#5. Godzilla vs. the Devil
This is another one based on a real concept. *Godzilla vs. the Devil* was seriously considered in 1978 as a U.S. Japan co-production along with a competing project, *Godzilla vs. Gargantua*.

"A prehistoric mastodon of destruction" rises from the earth to take on...

Frankenstein!

Godzilla fires his ray at...

Frankenstein!

First shot of the *Godzilla vs. the Devil* trailer.

Title card.

*A clawed hand from Monstroid.*

*Title character in Monstroid.*

*The spider from Magic Serpent was used instead of Kumonga from Son of Godzilla.*

*Another title card.*

*A hand reaches out for Godzilla. Is it the devil, or Titanosaurus?*

*One of the final title cards on Godzilla vs. the Devil.*

The maker of the *Godzilla vs. the Devil* trailer did their homework. Plot details for that film alleged that mankind's evil would spawn monsters in the form of a spider, a bird, and a fish—all of the giant variety, of course. The creator gets the first two courtesy of Toei's 1966 *The Magic Serpent*. This is an excellent choice over both Kumonga and the giant condor from Toho-land because it makes the trailer feel "new," so to speak.

For the fish monster, the creator used the strange mustachioed monster of *Monstroid* (1980). The trailer's other footage comes mostly from *Gamera vs. Gyaos*, but features neither of the titular creatures. A horror film with various, hooded cultists also features into the trailer, though I know not the source. The devil monster featured fits the mood also, but I don't know where it comes from.

The battle scenes are well edited. For instance, the editor takes a shot of the devil monster reaching towards something. We then cut to a red-tinted scene from *Terror of Mechagodzilla*, where Titanosaurus grabs Godzilla by the nose. Godzilla also faces off with the spider monster. Footage from *The Magic Serpent* is shown of it spraying its webbing, and then we see Godzilla getting sprayed by webbing (which belongs to Kumonga, naturally).

Overall this is one of the more believable fan trailers I've ever seen. Adding to this is the trailer's narration, lifted from *Godzilla vs. Megalon*, which works very well. The voice is distorted to make it sound creepier too.

### #4 Star Godzilla

In the late 1970s appeared an ad in *Variety* for *Star Godzilla*, a Hong Kong Godzilla movie produced by First Films distributers. The poster featured Godzilla, the De Laurentiis King Kong, and Anguirus. A UFO was also present. The production was real, proof of this was the ad and the fact that Toho made sure it got kyboshed right away. To this day, no one knows what it was about.

This is another of those trailers where the maker did their homework, as it begins with the First Films logo. It's then followed with brand new never before seen 70s Godzilla footage (not *Zone Fighter* either!). What was this miraculous footage, you ask? Well, it was really Haruo Nakajima's last jaunt in a Godzilla suit (which took place in a playground) in 1983 for a photoshoot for *Uchusen* magazine. Though incredibly cheesy (the suit was a 1979-built attraction suit for publicity purposes only), fans who didn't know any better could mistake this for new Godzilla footage.

After this new Godzilla footage we get an onslaught of destruction scenes courtesy of *Submersion of Japan* and the 1970s Godzilla movies. "NEW EXCITEMENT! NEW THRILLS!" The trailer proclaims over a volcano erupting. For a novice tokusatsu fan unfamiliar with more obscure movies, this trailer could almost trick you.

The editor inserts footage from *Super Infra-Man* (1975), notably the giant bug, and text screams, "INTRO-DUCING ROACHRA". Because the *Star Godzilla* poster had Kong, or at least a giant ape, the giant gorilla from *A\*P\*E* (1976) is inserted next. A few shots of Princess Dragon Mom pop up next, giving one the impression that perhaps she's an alien invader.

More "new" Godzilla footage comes next courtesy of a spoof scene from *One Crazy Summer* (1986). Then comes a giant snake

First Films logo.

Haruo Nakajima as Godzilla c.1979.

Shot from *Submersion of Japan*.

The bug monster from *Super Inframan*.

Shot from *A\*P\*E*.

Mosler, the "Horrible Snake."

The film's real tagline.

Footage from *Zone Fighter*.

49/THE LOST FILMS FANZINE #1

The Jellar brothers in *Zone Fighter*.

New York before being obliterated.

London before the explosion.

Who's that monster? Why it's Zarkorr, of course!

Well, it would have if not for legal reasons...

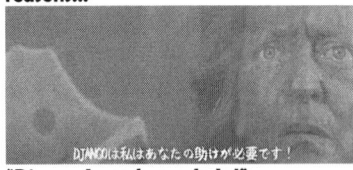

"Django I need your help!"

"What do you need me to do?"

Travel into the future!?

attacking a city that looks very much like 1970s era tokusatsu to someone who doesn't know better (it was from 1984's *King of Snake* AKA *Thunder of Gigantic Serpent*). Next up giant robots from one of the *Super Robot Red Baron* series pops up and then comes Godzilla to save the day via *Zone Fighter* (which again, looks like "new" footage to someone who's not aware that Godzilla guest-starred on the series). As Godzilla roars, the tagline for the movie that appeared on the poster flashes across the screen "Where the old world and the new world meet."

Then, "Star Godzilla vs. the Space Monsters" as Godzilla battles Jellar from *Zone Fighter*. After some more *Zone Fighter* footage, the major cities of the world are destroyed by way of stock footage from *The Last War* (1961) as it appeared in *The War in Space* (1977).

Next, the star of *Zarkorr: The Invader* (1996) pops up as "Star Godzilla's Greatest Foe." Since that monster was also suitmation, it seems plausible to show up in a Godzilla movie. The trailer ends with a happy shot of Godzilla that proclaims, "Coming Soon."

Considering that some people believe that some footage of *Star Godzilla* was shot (it wasn't that we know of) this trailer has the best odds of fooling someone into thinking it's real. Good job!

**#3. Django And Trinity Against Godzilla (1972)** The concept might sound ludicrous, but the trailer is edited so skillfully that it makes you want to see this movie—even if you're not already a Godzilla/Spaghetti Western fan!

What makes this trailer greater than it should be is just how professionally it is edited. We begin on the Toho Logo, while in the background we can hear a desolate wind. We cut to the deserted, muddy town from *Django* (1966), the most famous Spaghetti Western ever made outside of the Leone films. We see Franco Nero as Django, and then an old woman asks him for help. Cue the Japanese trailer for *Django*, complete with the famous Django theme song as Nero begins mowing down bad guys.

"What exactly do you need me to do?" Django asks. Cut to a stormy sky to classic Ifukube music from *Battle in Outer Space* (1959)/ *Godzilla vs. Gigan* (1972). As the music takes on a mysterious turn, we cut to the woman, then to Django. The image of Django is overlaid with a psychedelic effect that looks like the time travel from *Godzilla vs. King Ghidorah* (1991).

The next shot appears to show *Gigan's* Gengo and Shosaku observing Django arriving in 1972 dragging his coffin. Cue Godzilla climbing out of Tokyo Bay from *Destroy All Monsters* (1968). Godzilla's theme plays as he destroys the city while Django appears to watch. Then he busts out his signature Gatling gun (that's what he carries in the coffin, if you didn't know) and begins shooting at Godzilla (the *DAM* Tokyo military assault is used to represent this and it works).

Godzilla fires his ray, and we cut to a broken Django who rasps, "I can't kill Godzilla alone." Cue the mysterious old woman (it's clear to me she's somehow the one who sent Django through time), and then we cut to Terence Hill's Trinity character, complete with his catchy theme song. Due to Trinity's emergence, the trailer takes on a slightly comical tone (the Trinity films were comedies, after all). Django asks Trinity who he is, and

**Gengo and Shosaku meet...**

**Django in 1972!**

**He's there to fight Godzilla!**

**Django shoots...**

**At the King of the Monsters!**

**That didn't go well.**

**Better call for...**

**Trinity!!!**

51/THE LOST FILMS FANZINE #1

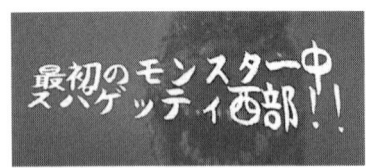

**Godzilla roars to the Django theme.**

**Trinity shoots...**

**Final frame of trailer.**

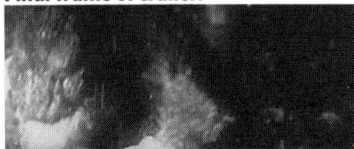

**Godzilla stirs...**

**Godzilla advances on a dam.**

**The dam breaks!**

**New destruction.**

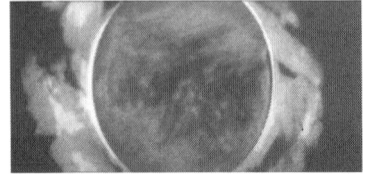

**Mysterious solar flare!**

real audio from a Terence Hill movie is used where his traditional dubber says, "Well, I'm gonna help you kill a monster."

The rest of the trailer is an action mashup, and one of the better bits appears to show Trinity shooting Godzilla in the face with a shotgun. During the final frames, the actors get their dues, with a close up on Franco as he says, "I'm just here to kill Godzilla." In another real audio clip, Trinity responds, "Biggest guy I ever saw."

The Django theme, now in Japanese, begins as we watch Godzilla roar. Trinity then shoots him in the shoulder courtesy of the scene with Gigan's buzz saw (sans Gigan, of course, we simply see Godzilla spurt blood and raise his arm). The final shots comprise of Godzilla to the Japanese Django music.

Whether you like the genre mashup or not, you have to admit it's an amazing trailer.

### #2 Godzilla Appears in Edo

I assume this idea was inspired by the lost film *King Kong Appears in Edo*, though I don't know that for sure. The only other person who's officially thrown around the notion of Godzilla appearing in Edo was *TMG* writer Yukiko Takayama, who said in an interview if she ever wrote another Godzilla script that would be her choice of story. Toho also almost did a Mothra movie (*Mothra 3*) where the big bug went back in time to Feudal Japan to battle a fire monster that was scrapped in favor of fighting King Ghidorah in the Cretaceous.

*Godzilla Appears in Edo*, more so than any fan trailer up to this point, looks like a period trailer from 1960s/1970s Japan. The direction is superb. It does its best to use "new" shots of Godzilla in the form

52/THE LOST FILMS FANZINE #1

of various SPFX outtakes. The first one we see is an unused take of Godzilla rising out of the water from *Son of Godzilla*. This is followed by a color corrected shot from *Mothra vs. Godzilla*. Next, we then see the Mosugoji style Godzilla advancing on a dam. No, this isn't an outtake either. We are now in unique territory, because this is a new composite shot created by the editor, Scott David Lister.

The dam breaks causing a massive flood. Some military music begins to play, and before we know it, Godzilla is fighting the Gohten! We then cut to the famous satellite station seen in *The Mysterians* and *Battle in Outer Space* as the Planet X theme plays. Something strange is going on. A solar flare destroys the base and creates a time-slip that sends Godzilla and the Gohten back in time!

We cut to a Japanese folk dance (Fujichiyo from *The Human Vapor*) along with period music to establish we are now back in time. We see a shot of a feudal village, and then Godzilla approaches through some trees (via footage from *Destroy All Monsters* when he chases Captain Yamabe at Mt. Fuji). The track from *Son of Godzilla's* final battle plays as Godzilla fires his atomic ray, destroying part of the town.

To the same score, we cut to an old sailing ship at sea which is attacked by Ebirah. The music and mood of the trailer changes as we focus back on the Feudal village. Gengo and Shosaku show up there (this is done because the duo visits an old style folk village that could pass for the Edo period in *Godzilla vs. Gigan*). The trailer notes that these two men are from the future as well.

We then cut to a sequence that makes it appear as though Godzilla is destroying Osaka castle. (Not the castle in Nagoya from *Mothra vs.*

**Time slip!!!**

**Godzilla caught in the time slip.**

**And the Gohten too!**

**Godzilla fires at the feudal village...**

**And destroys it!**

**An old sailing ship encounters...**

**Ebirah!**

**Feudal village.**

53/THE LOST FILMS FANZINE #1

**Gengo and Shosaku in Feudal Japan.**

**Nanbara then...**

**Nanbara now!**

**Godzilla vs. King Seesar.**

**Godzilla blasts some Samurai.**

**Samurai archers fire at Godzilla.**

**Godzilla fires!**

**The castle erupts in flames.**

*Godzilla*. I believe the footage of the castle breaking comes from *Gamera vs. Barugon* or *Gamera vs. Gyaos*.)

The plot continues to thicken as we cut to actor Shin Kishida, who played Nanbara in *Godzilla vs. Mechagodzilla* (1974). Here he is in feudal era clothing, but black and white flash-forwards also show Nanbara, so perhaps he's meant to either be an ancestor of Nanbara's or Nanbara in a past life?

Next comes my favorite aspect of all. First off, in case you haven't figured it out, this is the bad Godzilla pre-*Ghidorah, the Three-Headed Monster* we're dealing with. And, as a bad monster, he ends up tussling with none other than King Seesar via an excellent composite shot that makes it look as though the two kaiju are squaring off.

Next, Godzilla fights a whole army of Samurai in an exceptionally well cut scene. Suddenly an earthquake occurs (remember, the earthquake in *The Mysterians* destroyed some ancient structures) and suddenly Anguirus pops up!

Next thing we know, Rodan and King Ghidorah begin destroying feudal Japan too. Next, we check back in with the Gohten, and via some red-tinted lighting, Gengo appears to be on board. Then the Gohten appears to fire on Ebirah.

The trailer crescendos into a melee of action to frenetic Ifukube music where Anguirus fights Ghidorah, Mothra shows up, Godzilla fights King Seesar some more, and the Samurai just keep exploding. It ends on the image of a burning castle followed by a "Coming Soon" in Japanese.

Obviously, Lister may have made up the story around existing footage, but it's still a story I would like to see one day!

54/THE LOST FILMS FANZINE #1

## #1 Godzilla 1977

Initially, I thought this was a nod to the alleged 1977 *Godzilla* color remake (no, not the Luigi Cozzi one, the one Toho was supposedly going to produce). Instead, this trailer is meant to be a sequel to *Terror of Mechagodzilla*. It opens exceptionally, with the Godzilla theme, Toho logo, and then a rather creepy POV shot of Godzilla taken from the opening of *Son of Godzilla*. The 70s Godzilla shows up next and then blasts Tokyo with his ray. A very well done title with period appropriate lettering reading "Godzilla 77" in Japanese is overlaid over the exploding buildings.

Our next shot takes us to Monster Land in a long exterior shot, then shots denoting the film's real stars Godzilla (from *TMG*), Anguirus and Rodan (*DAM*). Then we get to the "people parts," which appears to show Gengo from *Gigan* spying Agent Nanbara from *Mechagodzilla*. Next up Gengo is meeting with Tamura and Murakoshi from *TMG* within Miyajima Labs and spouting off about alien invaders and monsters. (From this I gather Nanbara brought him there to meet the men). Cue an explosion and then a brand new shot: Hedorah walking across the moon!

Yoshimitsu Banno was planning to bring back Hedorah in 1975 anyways, so it fits. From the shot I surmise that Hedorah is attacking the moon base from *DAM*, but I'm not sure. Regardless of what he's attacking, he does attack via Ghidorah's rays. The shots are taken from *Invasion of Astro-Monster* and are colored red as Hedorah shoots his beam across the moon (really Planet X).

Suddenly, Godzilla is fighting a disguised Mechagodzilla again—repetitive, you say? Maybe, but did you know *TMG* originally was going

**Our first glimpse of Godzilla.**

**Hedorah on the moon!**

**Mechagodzilla 3 reveals itself.**

**MG3 in the air.**

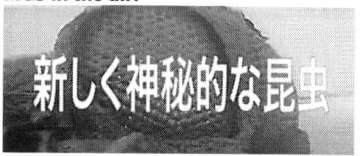

**A new monster, but who is it?**

**It's Battra!**

**Is Hedorah the big bad?**

**Final title card.**

55/THE LOST FILMS FANZINE #1

to repeat this gimmick too? We then get the alternate angle of Mechagodzilla's reveal from the 1974 trailer and then Mechagodzilla flying through the air with new text denoting him as MG3! And then, accompanied by Masaru Sato's frenetic music, Battra shows up! But doesn't that ruin the trailer's period atmosphere? No, because it's not really Battra, but a giant dragonfly from another production (read the interview to find out from where).

From Battra, we cut to Nanbara smoking on deck, and then Katsura answering the phone (she got rebuilt I'm guessing?) and on the other line is Gengo (remember, both characters have telephone scenes in their respective films). It's very well edited and not goofy in the least; it seems as though the two characters have a nervous flirtation going on.

We switch gears again into high action (Masaru Sato's jazzy *Ebirah* score plays) as Rodan destroys the oil refinery from *Mechagodzilla* via more composite work! Someone then kicks Anguirus high into the air (by reversing a shot of him falling to the ground in *DAM*). Gigan and Titanosaurus are revealed, and following this, some of the best human action scenes from the 1970s era films are intercut superbly to the Sato score.

In one of the most fun reveals, MG3 unloads his missiles onto Titanosaurus! I take this to mean the once peaceful dinosaur is now one of the good guys. We get one more shot of Hedorah (implying him to be the big bad), and then the burning oil refinery overlaid with the title again and Godzilla's roar.

Overall, the trailer has the zany pacing of a 1970s era trailer to a tee in terms of its music and direction. Nor is it overstuffed and shows some restraint in terms of plot (which I assume is a follow-up to *DAM*). Though it was a tough draw between *Godzilla '77* and *Godzilla Appears in Edo*, I think the former takes the cake!

**STOP PRESS!!!!!**
Just as this issue was going to print, Big Jack Films debuted a fantastic *Godzilla vs. King Kong* (1991) trailer using footage from *Godzilla vs. King Ghidorah* (1991), *King Kong* (1976), and *King Kong Lives* (1986). Had I seen it earlier, it would've made the top 2 easily. Check it out on YouTube now!

## AN INTERVIEW WITH SCOTT DAVID LISTER

**Scott David Lister is the talented editor behind three of the trailers on this list: *Godzilla and the Deadly Four*; *Godzilla Appears in Edo*, and *Godzilla '77*. Read on to learn more about his creative process as well as other projects he's worked on...**

**First off, I absolutely love your trailers, and in my opinion they are easily the best of the best. What inspired you to create them?**

Thank you so much! I'm so glad they're being appreciated. I've always been interested in film, and I've worked as an editor for several years now. In the Final Box DVD set, there's a reel of deleted SFX footage which I had never seen before. There are already a lot of fan trailers out there which use footage from the films that we're all familiar with, so I thought, if I made something mostly out of the deleted scenes, and the alternate takes in the trailers, maybe I could make something creatively fun and interesting. *Godzilla vs The Devil* was a big inspiration, as far as other fan trailers go. It conveys its own narrative and uses footage from other films to make something unique. The shot where the Devil reaches out and grabs Godzilla, and it uses a shot of Godzilla being grabbed by Titanosaurus tinted red, struck me as really clever. I thought, I'd love to create something like this!

**What was your inspiration for *Godzilla '77* specifically?**

I've always loved the 70's films. *Mechagodzilla '74* is possibly my all-time favourite Godzilla movie. I just wanted to celebrate one of my favourite eras of the series. The 60's got to go out with a bang with *Destroy All Monsters*. I thought, if they'd managed one last hurrah in the 70's, this is the kind of thing I would have loved to have seen. Something that brings everything back to cap off the era, like the final episode of *Ultraman Tiga*.

**In *Godzilla '77*, are the characters of Katsura Mifune and Gengo Kotaka meant to be returning, or just the actors that played them?**

Yes, those are meant to be the characters themselves coming back. I figured that if the 70's monsters were returning, it would be fun to cross over the 70's human characters as well, so you have Gengo meeting the *ToMG* Interpol guys at Miyajima's lab to discuss Monster Island, and stuff like that. You see fan trailers sometimes which focus on nothing but monsters, and that never really sells it for me, because no movie has ever been made without any human protagonists. I figured this Katsura had been rebuilt to be more benevolent. I chose Gengo for the lead because he comes off like a goofy everyman caught in this crazy situation, and that's so endearing.

**In your mind, what is the basic storyline in your head for *Godzilla '77*? I think I can pick out certain elements, like Titanosaurus is apparently a good guy now who fights Mechagodzilla III, etc.**

Yeah, that detail just kind of came up in the edit. There's an unused shot of MG in front of an exploding mountain from the deleted footage, and it just seemed to work being juxtaposed with Titanosaurus.

At the end of the 70's, Hedorah appears on the moon, and then MGIII attacks Japan disguised as the real Godzilla. It soon becomes apparent these aren't freak occurrences; unseen aliens are attacking the Earth with an army of monsters, and have also sealed Monster Island off with a force field so that none of Earth's monsters can defend against them. Katsura, having been rebuilt and now on the side of the humans, tries to fend the monsters off with Titanosaurus, but he's outmatched. The Interpol agents seek out Gengo and conspire to free Godzilla, Rodan and Angilas from Monster Island to fight off the invading monsters.

**Where did some of the non-Godzilla footage come from? Your new version of Battra, for instance?**

It was so fun that it took a while for the comments section to pick where Battra was from! He's from a 1973 episode of *Doctor Who* called "The

Green Death." Classic Who is my other big love next to Godzilla from when I was a child, and the time period just seemed to fit! The funny thing is that that monster is barely even human-sized, and it's defeated by Jon Pertwee throwing his coat at it.

*Edo* actually has much more footage from non-G movies. Since it was the second trailer and I'd exhausted a lot of the Final Box footage, I wanted to really try to give people something they hadn't seen before in a Godzilla context. The opening sunrise shot is from Bruce Lee's *The Big Boss* (1971), there's an exploding hut from *Incident at Blood Pass* (1970), most of the war scenes are from the original *Sengoku Jietai/GI Samurai* (1979), there's a bit of *Zatoichi Meets Yojimbo* (1970), the closing shot is from Kurosawa's *Ran* (1985)... Most of the dam/power plant exploding sequence is from an Antonio Margheriti film called *Killer Fish* (1979). He was a master at doing miniature explosions, as that sequence shows. I included so much of it because I wanted to show to Godzilla fans just how amazing his work was. He also did a kind of monster movie in the late 80s, called *Alien From The Deep* (1989), about a giant underground alien monster destroying a power plant. He didn't have as much money on that one as *Killer Fish*, but when it gets going it's a lot of fun. Gave me nightmares when I was a child!

**How were the shots of Hedorah on the moon and Rodan attacking the oil refinery created?**

I did them in Adobe After Effects, by cutting out and overlaying different pieces of footage, like a collage. The Hedorah sequence is a mix of footage of Planet X with Ghidorah's rays turned red, plus the exploding lunar surface from *Destroy All Monsters*. The shots of Hedorah on Mt. Fuji had no real background, just a black sky, so it was easy to put Planet X mountains in front of him and composite him in. Same with Rodan at the oil refinery, he was just flying against a blue backdrop, so it was easy to pull the sky out. I wanted to include some kind of SFX shots which wouldn't be immediately identifiable, to give the trailer its own flavour, and make people go, "where on earth is that from?"

At the time, I made them on my old laptop, and it was really slow and somewhat tricky to do. That's why there's only a few of them. These days, I'm better at compositing and I have a much more powerful setup, so I could probably do an entire trailer of shots like that.

**Moving onto *Godzilla in Edo*, I get the impression that the story is set during Godzilla's bad guy days of the early 1960s, am I correct?**

That's right! I figured; I'd already done Hero Godzilla in the '77 trailer. To have Godzilla travel back in time and be benevolent and not fight anybody just wouldn't make sense! Plus, 60s footage just seemed to match better with the feudal period. I love the idea of Godzilla or other monsters appearing in other locations or situations. I want to see Godzilla or other monsters in a desert, or an icy tundra, among the pyramids in Egypt, or deep in the jungle. I feel like since the 90's we've just had monsters showing up in contemporary cities again and again for the most part.

**Furthermore, what is your idea of the overall storyline for this**

project? Is the idea that Shin Kishida's character is Agent Nanbara in a past life?

Bingo - I'm glad these ideas actually come across! So, Godzilla attacks a dam and a power plant in modern Japan, and the Gotengo is dispatched after him. But right above them, a satellite malfunctions and explodes, causing a rift in time which sucks Godzilla, the Gotengo, a bunch of other monsters and the human characters (Gengo and Shosaku) back to feudal Japan. Gengo and Shosaku encounter past versions of Tomoko Tomoe and Agent Nanbara (who has a plan to fight the monsters by awakening King Seesar), and have to join the Gotengo crew to fight through the monsters and somehow return home.

**Considering there are now over thirty G-films, you would think that Toho would've made one with Godzilla in feudal Japan. Are you aware that Yukiko Takayama also came up with a story concept for a similar idea? If so, did that inspire you in any way to create the Edo trailer?**

I actually had no idea! I'd be very curious to hear what her concept was. I'm sure it was probably suitably tragic, haha. My inspiration, if anything, was of course the lost film *King Kong Appears In Edo* (1938). Also, watching *GI Samurai*, and the combination of feudal war scenes with explosions and some light tokusatsu, made me think of how obvious it would be to include Godzilla. You're right that it's an obvious concept which is strange to have not been explored. That's probably why I went with it really!

You show a lot more restraint in your fan trailers than other editors do. Some of them throw in too many elements to where it loses any semblance of a real movie trailer. What were some of the discarded ideas you restrained yourself from including in both *Godzilla '77* and *Edo*?

Well, thank you! They're fairly crazy, but I always tried to keep the story in mind, and imagine, "could I picture this many details in an actual film?" If not, then out it went. Originally, I was going to have the Gotengo in G'77, via footage from *The War In Space* (1977). The timeline of course fits perfectly, but it just seemed overstuffed. Luckily, I realized I could bring that idea back in *Edo*. I wanted Baragon, and I thought about Redmoon and Ebarus, but again, it all seemed like too much. The detail of Hedorah appearing initially on the moon was somewhat inspired by *Godzilla vs Redmoon*, so that survived, at least. I toyed with including some *Zone Fighter* footage, but my copies of the episodes weren't good enough quality. I think there was a shot of Rodan actually fighting Hedorah at the refinery after he flies over it, which just didn't look good; it was an awful composite, so I dropped it. I cut a few little scenes of monsters interacting and fighting - I ended up whittling it down to just the best ones. So, it was just a process of elimination, of keeping things reasonable and only retaining the best elements.

*Edo* had much less cut out – I think I might have originally thought about including Gigan or MechaGodzilla, but overall there wasn't a whole lot to lose, because by that point I had a pretty good idea of how to stay focused and streamlined. There was much less footage that looked like ancient Japan, so it was much more a process of "what shots will work with this concept?"

**You've recently expanded beyond fan trailers and are now doing a web-series called *Unbalance*. I take it that's based upon the Tsuburaya TV series concept called *Unbalance*?**

It is, very loosely! It's an *Ultra Q*-type show, with giant monsters, human-sized creatures, a bit of cartoony violence, some weird sci-fi concepts about different dimensions, and even a bit of martial arts. It's all very lo-fi, I basically made it to try doing certain special effects and ideas, and to just showcase everything I'm into. We did about half a dozen ten-minute episodes.

The first two episodes set up the story, and are about a giant Godzilla-like monster called Mogu, who is based very loosely on the unused kaiju from the unmade *The Return of King Ghidorah*. The next three parts are kind of a combination of *The H-Man*, *From Hell It Came*, and the *Doctor Who* story "The Power of Kroll," with a blood-drinking plant monster which invades a nightclub to eat the dancers and eventually becomes gigantic.

I still haven't released *Unbalance*, but it was filmed a while ago, so it'll be out soon. But I've gone on to other things since – I've made a few horror and sci-fi shorts, and I'm currently developing a sci-fi action feature film. So the future is hopefully bright!

**Any other Japanese fan trailers in the future I hope?**

I think so! I'd love to do something even wilder. Like I said, I'm much better with After Effects now, so I'd like to do a trailer that is almost entirely done that way. One concept I love is of combining Godzilla with a 60's or 70's spy movie or show, like *ESPY* or *Flower Action 009-1*. Another idea I've had for a long time is to actually film some original human scenes, do them in widescreen and make them look old and grainy, and make a "new" Godzilla short or trailer using Showa FX scenes but new human footage. Like, you could film characters running away from Godzilla in a jungle, and edit in shots of Godzilla's feet stomping through Sollgel Island from *Son of Godzilla*. Things like that. So I definitely think I'll do more. The possibilities, even with this limited footage, are endless!

**NEXT ISSUE:**
THE LOST *KOLCHAK: THE NIGHT STALKER* MOVIES
BARAGON GOES BOLLYWOOD IN *AADI YUG*
CHRISTOPHER REEVE AND GERARD CHRISTOPHER AS THE MAN OF STEEL IN *SUPERMAN V: THE NEW MOVIE*
*MOONLIGHT MASK: THE MOVIE*
UNMADE SEQUELS TO *ORCA*
AND MORE!!!

Printed in Great Britain
by Amazon